DEC
Recommended Practices

in Early Intervention/Early Childhood
Special Education

Susan Sandall • **Mary E. McLean** • **Barbara J. Smith**

Proofreading by Raven Moore
Cover and Layout Design by Becky Malone

ISBN 1-57035-353-0

Disclaimer

Funding for this publication came in part from a grant to the University of Colorado at Denver and the Division for Early Childhood from the U.S. Department of Education, Office of Special Education Programs (grant no. H324D.980033). The contents of this book do not necessarily reflect the views or policies of the U.S. Department of Education or the University of Colorado at Denver.

IDEAs that Work
Office of Special Education Programs

Published and Distributed by:

SOPRIS
WEST

4093 Specialty Place
Longmont, CO 80504
(303) 651-2829
www.sopriswest.com

1380 Lawrence Street, Suite 650
Denver, CO 80204
(303) 556-3328
www.dec-sped.org

The Division for Early Childhood (DEC) of the Council for Exceptional Children (CEC) is a national, nonprofit organization of individuals who work with or on behalf of children with special needs, birth through age eight, and their families. Founded in 1973, DEC is dedicated to promoting policies and practices that support families and enhance the optimal development of children. Children with special needs include those who have disabilities, developmental delays, are gifted/talented, or are at risk of future developmental problems.

143REC/BAN/7-01/5M/302

Contributors

. . . .

Stephen J. Bagnato, Ed.D.
Children's Hospital of Pittsburgh
The UCLID Center at the University
    of Pittsburgh
3705 5th Avenue
Pittsburgh, PA 15213

Alison Broudy, M.A.
University of Colorado at Denver
Center for Collaborative
    Educational Leadership
DEC Recommended Practices Project
1380 Lawrence Street, Suite 650
Denver, CO 80204

Carl J. Dunst, Ph.D.
Orelena Hawks Puckett Institute
18A Regent Park Boulevard
Asheville, NC 28806

Gloria Harbin, Ph.D.
University of North Carolina
    at Chapel Hill
Frank Porter Graham
    Child Development Center
137 E. Franklin Street
Chapel Hill, NC 27514

Mary Louise Hemmeter, Ph.D.
University of Kentucky
Department of Special Education
229 Taylor Education Building
Lexington, KY 40506

Mary E. McLean, Ph.D.
University of Wisconsin-Milwaukee
Department of Exceptional Education
PO Box 413
Milwaukee, WI 53201

R.A. McWilliam, Ph.D.
University of North Carolina
    at Chapel Hill
Frank Porter Graham
    Child Development Center
CB #8180, 105 Smith Level Road
Chapel Hill, NC 27599

Patricia S. Miller, Ph.D.
College of Charleston
Special Education and Early Childhood
Charleston, SC 29424

John T. Neisworth, Ph.D.
Penn State University
Special Education Program
207 Cedar
University Park, PA 16802

Christine Salisbury, Ph.D.
University of Illinois-Chicago
College of Education
1640 W. Roosevelt Road
MC 628, IIDD 336
Chicago, IL 60608

Contributors

Susan Sandall, Ph.D.
University of Washington
Experimental Education Unit
Box 357925
Seattle, WA 98195

Rosa Milagros (Amy) Santos, Ph.D.
University of Illinois at Urbana-
    Champaign
Department of Special Education
61 Children's Research Center
51 Gerty Drive
Champaign, IL 61820

Barbara J. Smith, Ph.D.
Division for Early Childhood (DEC)
1380 Lawrence Street, Suite 650
Denver, CO 80204

Patricia Snyder, Ph.D.
Louisiana State University
Health Sciences Center
School of Allied Health Professions
1900 Gravier Street
New Orleans, LA 70112

Vicki D. Stayton, Ph.D.
Western Kentucky University
College of Education
    and Behavioral Sciences
#1 Big Red Way
Bowling Green, KY 42101

Kathleen Stremel, M.A.
Western Oregon University
Teaching Research
345 N. Monmouth Avenue
Monmouth, OR 97361

Carol M. Trivette, Ph.D.
Orelena Hawks Puckett Institute
128 S. Sterling Street
Morganton, NC 28655

Mark Wolery, Ph.D.
Vanderbilt University
Department of Special Education
Box 328 Peabody College
Nashville, TN 37203

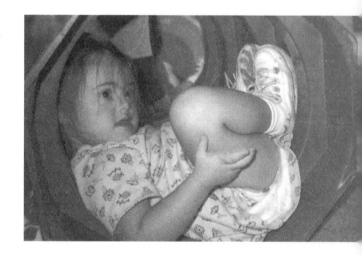

Acknowledgments

· · · · · · · · · · · ·

DEC wishes to recognize those who have given of their expertise, time, and resources to help identify recommended practices and to produce this book. First, we wish to acknowledge the vision, leadership, and hard work of the late Dr. David Sexton. As DEC Vice President, President Elect, and President, Dr. Sexton encouraged DEC to expand our products and training efforts in order to impact the quality of services and outcomes for young children with special needs and their families. In June 1998 he joined the editors of this book at the DEC Executive Offices in Denver, Colorado to write a grant proposal to the U.S. Department of Education that resulted in funding for the research efforts that led to the recommended practices and this book. In addition to serving on the Management Team of the project, Dr. Sexton also directed the project's extensive literature review activities associated with determining the scientific support for Early Intervention/Early Childhood Special Education practice. Dr. Sexton's colleagues at Louisiana State University Health Sciences Center, Marcia Lobman, Jeff Oremland, Sally Fussell, and Dr. Patricia Snyder, worked closely with him in the successful, albeit daunting, task of coordinating the review and coding of over 1,000 articles from 48 scientific journals. This book and the associated other products and training that will be available to the field as a result of Dr. Sexton's vision will contribute to the improvement of services to and outcomes for young children with special needs and their families for years to come.

In addition to the Project Investigators—Drs. David Sexton, Susan Sandall, Mary McLean, and Barbara J. Smith—this project benefitted from the continuous advice and assistance from Dr. Samuel L. Odom who served as liaison to the strand chairs, as a methodology consultant, and on the project's Management Team; and Dr. Bruce Thompson, Dr. Patricia Snyder, and Dr. Phillip S. Strain who also served as methodology consultants and as members of the Management Team. Thirteen experts in the field coordinated the work of the recommended practices strands: Drs. Stephen J. Bagnato, Mary Beth Bruder, Carl J. Dunst, Gloria Harbin, R.A. McWilliam, Patricia S. Miller, John T. Neisworth, Christine Salisbury, Rosa Milagros (Amy) Santos, Vicki D. Stayton, Kathleen Stremel, Carol M. Trivette, and Mark Wolery. Dr. Mary Louise Hemmeter joined the project during the second year as the project moved into outreach and dissemination activities.

Acknowledgments

Dedicated staff included University of Colorado at Denver—Alison Broudy, Linda Frederick, Julie Walden, and Carl Sumi; University of Washington—Joan Ronk and Kari Moe; and University of Wisconsin at Milwaukee—Becky Reimbold and Ali Faber.

Members of the DEC Executive Board, Committee Chairs, and Editors who served over the 2-year period of the project supported and, in some cases, directly assisted the effort. They are Lucinda Bernheimer, Patricia Blasco, Linda Brault, Jerry Christensen, Laurie Dinnebeil, Lourdes Gonzalez, Sarah Hadden, Mary Louise Hemmeter, Gail Joseph, Jennifer Kilgo, John Killoran, Maggie LaMontagne, Diana LaRocco, Rich Lewis, Susan McBride, Mary McEvoy, Mary McLean, R.A. McWilliam, Billie Navojosky, Micki Ostrosky, Philip Printz, Maurine Ballard-Rosa, Sharon Rosenkoetter, Beth Rous, Gwen Wheeler Russell, Susan Sandall, Amy Santos, David Sexton, Vicki D. Stayton, Judy Swett, Vicki Turbiville, Laura Vagianos, and Amy Whitehead.

Thanks, also, to the more than 370 individuals who completed the field validation survey, which contained 120 items!

Finally, approximately 150 other individuals participated and assisted in the project as focus group participants and literature review coders or validators. *These individuals are listed in Appendix A.*

Thank you to all these people who have taken time from their busy schedules to help DEC attempt to serve the early childhood community through recommending practices that should lead to better outcomes for young children with special needs and their families.

Contents

· · · · · · · · · · · ·

Contents

Images of Early Intervention/Early Childhood Special Education

. . . .

Teacher

. . . .

Steve pulls into a parking space at Walters School. He reaches in the back seat of his car for a plastic crate filled with file folders. As he walks through the door of the school he remembers that he once taught preschoolers in this building. Now he has a desk and file cabinets. He spends his days with children at many different schools, centers, and homes. Once or twice a day he stops in to exchange file folders, grab toys, and check his messages.

Today he spent most of the day at Green Tree, a child care center in a small town about 10 miles away. There are four children with disabilities enrolled at the center, and Steve is their itinerant early childhood special education teacher from the school district. Steve spent time watching the children, leading a couple of small group activities, reviewing notes, and talking with the teachers. He introduced one little boy to a picture schedule to help him participate in daily activities. It seemed like the schedule would help him so Steve demonstrated for the teacher, watched the teacher try it, and told her that he would check in with her in a few days.

During the children's naptime, Steve and one of the teachers phoned Jason's mother, Ms. Thomas, to see if they could arrange a meeting to review his IEP. They arrived at a few tentative times that Steve will confirm with the speech therapist and the school district's special education director. They also got to spend a few minutes comparing notes and delighting in Jason's growing vocabulary. Ms. Thomas said that she thinks that Jason's improving language has made a big difference in his behavior. Steve makes a note to himself and asks Ms. Thomas if she will share that information with the whole team at the IEP meeting.

Steve's caseload includes some children under the age of 3 whose early intervention program is administered by the county school district's office. Now Steve replaces file folders in his cabinet and retrieves a folder for one of those children, Emma. He will stop to see Emma and her family on his way home from work. Emma is 2 years old and has Down syndrome. She stays at home with her mother during the day. Emma's mother speaks primarily Vietnamese, and the family has requested that home visits be

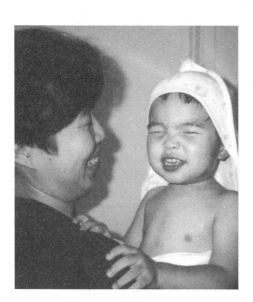

scheduled for the end of the work day so that Emma's father, who is bilingual, can participate. Steve looks forward to this visit. Emma recently began to walk, and home visits usually begin with a cheerful show of her new talent. Last week Emma's grandmother was at the home visit for the first time. Emma took turns taking steps to her mother, father, grandmother, and big sister. What a fun visit. This week Steve will bring the video camera and make a video that can be shared with the consulting physical therapist.

Steve often thinks about how much his job has changed. Sometimes, he misses his classroom. But working at child care centers and visiting homes has opened his eyes. He's glad his supervisor understands the time and energy this new job requires.

Family Member

Teri gives Anthony just one more kiss on the forehead; says good-bye to her sister, Kim; and then turns and opens the door. Cathy Johnson, the early intervention service coordinator, is sitting in her parked car waiting for Teri to come out of the house. Cathy is taking Teri to the IEP meeting at Prescott School. Long before Anthony's third birthday,

Teri had begun to worry about this day. This IEP meeting signaled the end of early intervention for Anthony and the beginning of services from the public schools. School! How could Anthony be going to school?

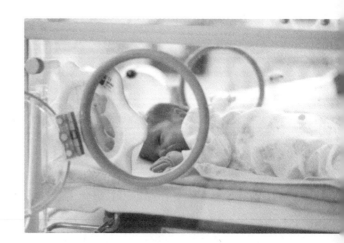

It is hard to believe that Anthony is almost 3 years old. Teri thought back to the night of his birth. The premature arrival of her little boy had changed everything in Teri's life. Not only did he arrive early, but also he was in the hospital for a long time.

When he finally did come home from the hospital, he was so little and fragile. He was still on a monitor, and Teri was afraid to go to sleep, thinking that the monitor would go off and she wouldn't wake up. Her sister and mother had helped her a lot during that time. That's also the time she first met Cathy, who works for the county's early intervention program. Cathy has been there almost from the beginning. Teri cannot imagine what it will be like when Cathy no longer comes to help her with Anthony.

That isn't the only change that Teri is facing. She has been accepted into a training program to become a nurse's aide. She will be in the next class to begin the program. Anthony isn't the only member of the family who is going to school! That's another reason that the IEP meeting is so important. Teri has to be certain that Anthony is happy and is getting everything he needs. Only then will she be able to concentrate on becoming a nurse's aide.

This IEP meeting is really important. Last week, Cathy told Teri that a lady from the school district wanted her to be on a special team that the school was putting together. Cathy said the school wanted to have the best early childhood services they could, and Teri was being asked to be one of the parents on this team that would learn about good programs and make suggestions for Anthony's school. Well, there won't be a lot of extra time in Teri's life once she starts the nurse's aide program. But how could she say no? This would give her the opportunity to see that Anthony, and other children too, would have the best possible services. Teri was going to find out more information about this team today.

Teri closes the door behind her and walks toward Cathy's car. She smiles to herself. It actually feels like more than an end to something. It feels like a beginning too . . . .

Administrator

As the new Director of Special Education for the Green Valley School District, Janice Logan is responsible for ensuring that all eligible children with disabilities receive a free appropriate public education (FAPE) as defined by federal and state laws and regulations. Until 5 years ago, none of the elementary schools served children under the age of five. Today they all do, using a variety of models including school-based segregated classrooms and community-based itinerant services.

Janice has little previous experience or training in early childhood. Like all administrators, Janice has more work to do than time or resources. When she was learning about her new job, she often faced a series of crises. However, since she didn't know much about early childhood services, she decided to focus for 4 months on learning more about how to appropriately serve the young children with disabilities and their families in her district. What Janice did know about early childhood was that high quality early experiences lead to better school outcomes.

During those months Janice did three things: (1) created a supervisory position in early childhood special education; (2) learned about early childhood practices that promote positive outcomes; and (3) identified early childhood/early childhood special education leaders, stakeholders, and resources either in the education system or in the community.

First, she talked with principals and learned that the National Association for Elementary School Principals as well as several other national organizations had position statements encouraging school districts to have a separate unit and supervisor to oversee educational programs for young children. Following that recommendation, the district had recently designed an early childhood unit and hired a supervisor who was

responsible for programs for children under the age of 8 including Title I; Even Start, the state funded preschool program; kindergarten; and 1st and 2nd grade. However, no one had thought to include special education services. Janice decided to hire an early childhood special educator (ECSE) to work with the early childhood education (ECE) supervisor and decided that the special education and related services needed by young children would be a collaborative effort of the special education and early childhood units.

Second, Janice improved her knowledge of effective practices for young children with disabilities and their families by hiring and learning from the ECSE supervisor. As she learned more, Janice encouraged and supported the purchase of materials and training related to implementing recommended practices in ECSE and ECE.

Third, Janice knew that in order to create new and improved services the district would need to make some changes. She knew about systems change since she had been involved in the restructuring of special education in her previous job. She knew that she had to bring individuals together to share in making systems change decisions. A team of individuals could share ideas, resources, and vision and create commitment to a new way of doing things. Janice invited the early childhood supervisor to co-sponsor the development of an early childhood recommended practices team of parents, teachers, related services personnel, and community administrators from Head Start and child care. She invited several parents including Teri, a new parent coming into the preschool program from the county's Part C program. She also invited Steve, an ECSE teacher who had been through the transition from classroom teacher to itinerant teacher. She invited Rena from the University. This team will begin meeting monthly to create a vision of including all children with disabilities in all early childhood services and programs. Janice also hopes that this team will begin to identify the key issues for the district and help identify some solutions.

Now, at the end of the 4 months, Janice knows more about high quality practices for improving outcomes for young children with disabilities and their families. She turns her attention to other areas of need knowing that the ECE and ECSE supervisors and the recommended practices team will monitor progress and let her know when they need her support.

Higher Education Faculty Member

Over the course of a week, Rena receives calls from a child care provider, a public school administrator, an early interventionist, and a Head Start director. They are all calling to inquire about the University's teacher education program in early childhood special education. The child care provider has suddenly found her center serving several children with disabilities, and there is no one on staff who has any experience working with these children or with their itinerant teachers. The early interventionist has just been hired and does not have the appropriate certification. The program has given her 1 year to complete the requirements. The Head Start Director is calling because of the new mandate requiring more advanced training for lead teachers. And Janice, the public school administrator, wants to talk about some ideas she has for retooling her current teachers.

While the early interventionist is calling about the teacher education program for herself, the Head Start Director and child care provider are inquiring about training opportunities for their staff. Rena describes the early childhood special education certification program including the entrance requirements, courses and field experiences, and the student teaching requirement. While the certification program meets the needs of some of the people who have called, it does not work for all of them.

In fact, Rena and Janice, the public school administrator, have a long conversation about the curriculum itself and whether or not it addresses the needs of teachers who will spend a great deal of time working with other adults. Janice tells her that several of the district's preschool teachers are reluctant to leave their classrooms for itinerant positions.

In addition, the callers tell her that the schedule and location of the courses often conflict with work schedules. Sometimes the entrance requirements and/or prerequisites prevent individuals from enrolling, and the program is too lengthy to meet the immediate needs of some individuals. Rena tries her best to help the callers identify alternative options.

At the next early childhood faculty meeting, Rena discusses the issues that have been raised in her conversations with these and other early childhood professionals. The faculty has grown increasingly aware of the diverse needs of individuals pursuing educational opportunities in the field of early childhood special education. They are committed to working with the various early childhood systems that provide services to young children with disabilities and their families. They realize that they are going to have to look at a variety of options including distance learning, evening and weekend courses, on-site training and technical assistance, and alternative routes to certification. They have a big job ahead of them.

Rena, Janice, Teri, and Steve all find themselves in the midst of the changing field of Early Intervention/Early Childhood Special Education. They have a wealth of knowledge and skills, but they find themselves searching for new ways to meet today's challenges. Our hope is that DEC Recommended Practices in Early Intervention/Early Childhood Special Education will provide information and direction for meeting these challenges.

Introduction to the DEC Recommended Practices

. . . .

Susan Sandall and Barbara J. Smith

The stories in *Images of Early Intervention/Early Childhood Special Education* provide glimpses of the challenges, complexities, and rewards of living and working with young children with disabilities. Families and educators share the goal of improved development and learning outcomes for these children. The meanings we attach to such outcomes—improved social competence, independence, and problem solving and enhanced family functioning—may differ. The methods we use to reach the outcomes may vary based on our knowledge and beliefs. The purpose of this book is to provide guidance on effective practices for attaining our shared goal for young children with disabilities and their families.

The Division for Early Childhood (DEC) of the Council for Exceptional Children (CEC) is dedicated to promoting policies and practices that support families and enhance the optimal development of children. One of the responsibilities of the organization is to define and facilitate recommended practices related to young children with disabilities.

Evidence from a variety of sources supports the connection between early learning experiences and later school and work performance. In this book we bring together those guiding, recommended practices—based on research and shared beliefs—to help educators, other practitioners, families, and administrators provide quality learning experiences.

At the beginning of the 1990s, several members of DEC undertook a project to identify recommended practices in early intervention/early childhood special education. The practices were compiled in two products: a DEC document first published in 1993 (DEC Task Force on Recommended Practices, 1993) and a book that extended the underlying concepts (Odom & McLean, 1996).

Photo by David Naylor

As the 20th century drew to a close, we asked several questions including, "Are the practices current?" "What else have we learned?" and "Are the practices being used?" We realized that widespread adoption of the practices had not occurred. We wondered why and arrived at three possible challenges to widespread adoption. First, the practices did not have a current and thorough synthesis of the knowledge base. Second, we had not done an adequate job of translating and disseminating the information to those individuals who have the actual responsibility for educating young children. Third, we had not fully appreciated the administrative and systems change supports that are necessary for the sustained delivery of high-quality services to children and their families.

Inspired by the goal of improved outcomes for young children with disabilities and their families, we designed a new project to review the research literature, integrate the literature with those practices identified as critical by our various stakeholders, develop and disseminate user-friendly products, and address the administrative and systems change foundations necessary for long-term adoption and use of quality practices.

This book is the first product in a series of materials and activities aimed at bridging the gap between research and practice. Our primary goal was to identify practices that are related to better outcomes for young children with disabilities, their families, and the

The DEC Recommended Practices focus on young children who are eligible for early intervention/early childhood special education services and their families. For purposes of this book, early intervention (EI) refers to services and supports for children under the age of 3 years. Early childhood special education (ECSE) refers to services and supports for children ages 3 through 5 years. Services for young children and their families include a range of educational, developmental, and therapeutic activities. Supports include support networks of family, friends, and others; more formal supports in the form of public services; and the other relationships that help families maintain their central role as caregivers and acquire new knowledge and skills. By supports we also mean those administrative and personnel supports that can help ensure that quality services are provided.

personnel who serve them. We identified the practices through focus groups of stake-holders: practitioners, personnel trainers, researchers, administrators, and family members. These practices were integrated with those found from our extensive review of the literature. The resulting practices underwent a field validation. (More information about the process is found in Chapter 9.) With this book, the other materials that will follow, and other DEC resources and initiatives, we hope to provide guidance to the field that will result in positive changes in child development and learning, family functioning, and attitudes attributed to services and supports for children from birth through 5 with disabilities, their families, and the personnel who serve them.

References

Division for Early Childhood Task Force on Recommended Practices. (Eds.). (1993). *DEC recommended practices: Indicators of quality in programs for infants and young children with special needs and their families.* Reston, VA: Council for Exceptional Children.

Odom, S.L., & McLean, M.E. (1996). *Early intervention/early childhood special education: Recommended practices.* Austin, TX: PRO-ED.

Notes

Chapter 1

DEC's New Recommended Practices: The Context for Change

· · · · · · · · · · · ·

Susan Sandall, Mary E. McLean, Rosa Milagros (Amy) Santos, and Barbara J. Smith

DEC's Recommended Practices are based on two key sources. One source is the scientific literature on effective practices for young children with disabilities, their families, and the personnel who work with them. The second source is the knowledge and experience of researchers and other stakeholders. That is, the practices are based on a current synthesis of scientific *and* experiential knowledge. Still, there are other contextual variables that influence the practices. In this chapter we examine some of those influences. We end the chapter by describing the organization of the remaining sections of the book.

A basic premise underlying the definition and dissemination of recommended practices is recognition of the relationship between early experiences and later outcomes. There is a clear link between the quality of an early childhood program and child outcomes (Bryant, Burchinal, Lau, & Sparling, 1994; Burchinal, Lee, & Ramey, 1989; Burchinal, Roberts, Nabors, & Bryant, 1996; Buysse & Bailey, 1993; Cost, Quality, & Child Outcomes Study Team, 1995; Howes, Phillips, & Whitebook, 1992). Defining recommended practices for the field of EI/ECSE is guided by an intention to identify practices that result in quality programs and thus have a positive impact on both child and family outcomes.

The Changing Nature of Early Intervention and Education

· · · · · · · · · · · · · · · ·

Early intervention and early childhood special education have been shaped by history, legislation, and by society's changing views about young children with disabilities and other special needs and their families. We often trace our historical roots to the early nonprofit efforts in communities as well as to the establishment of federally-funded model demonstration programs for young children in the late 1960s. The model programs, first funded by the Bureau of Education for the Handicapped of the U.S. Department of Education, were created to demonstrate the feasibility of various models for serving young children with disabilities. These programs (over 600 have been funded) have exerted a strong influence on the *look* of early intervention/early childhood special education (EI/ECSE). However, model programs only reach some children. Federal law extended the reach to all children with disabilities in 1986 (Hebbeler, Smith, & Black, 1991).

The legislative history dates back to a few state laws passed in the 1970s, the passage in 1975 of a federal law, Public Law 94-142, now known as Part B of the Individuals with Disabilities Education Act (IDEA), and the 1986 amendments to IDEA. Though PL 94-142 was focused primarily on special education and related services for school-aged children, the law was designed to apply to children ages 3 through 5 if state laws included this group. The basic tenets of this landmark legislation were free and appropriate public education (FAPE); zero reject; individualized education; nondiscriminatory testing, classification, and placement; least restrictive environment; rights to procedural due process; and shared decision making. In 1986, Congress amended IDEA and ensured these important rights to young children and their families. This law (PL 99-457) extended all of the rights and protections of the earlier law to children with disabilities ages 3 through 5 regardless of state age limits. In addition, the law included important incentives to states to provide services for infants and toddlers (birth through age 2) with disabilities and their families. IDEA, along with other legislation and state and local policies, has had a significant impact on the services and supports young children with disabilities and their families receive.

Photo by David Naylor

Societal views also influence early intervention/early childhood special education. Knowledge and perspectives about children and families change, and our programs and practices reflect this. First, there is heightened awareness of the importance of the child's early years on development and learning. Due, in part, to the remarkable findings of brain researchers (see Diamond & Hopson, 1999; Shore, 1997), we know that during the early years, brain cells form most of the connections that they will maintain throughout a child's lifetime. During this same period, brain cells maintain their greatest malleability. Healthy early brain development is central to establishing developmental trajectories that are conducive to children's optimal learning and development. Further, it is during these early years that children develop attitudes toward learning.

Knowledge and perspectives about children and families change, and our programs and practices reflect this.

Second, there is heightened awareness of the need for quality care for young children. We know that there is a critical link between early experiences and later performance in school and in the community. Recent studies show that the quality of children's early experiences in child care matters more than experts had previously thought (Child Care Action Campaign, 2000). Unfortunately, quality early care is not always guaranteed, and yet the demand for care is increasing.

Third, there is heightened awareness of the rights of children with disabilities to have access to child care, education, and recreational activities (see Appendix B). There is growing awareness of the importance of participation and membership for a full and meaningful life. Within families and communities, young children with disabilities are increasingly included in the same settings and activities where we find their brothers, sisters, and typical peers. Young children with disabilities have a right to be included and to be supported in their families and communities.

Thus any attempt to define and share guidance about the practices that should be in place for young children with disabilities is influenced by our history, legislation, and the societal context and values in which the practices are identified. Early intervention/early childhood special education is an ever-changing field. The guidance offered in these practices incorporates current knowledge from the research literature and integrates that knowledge with important values.

Our Values and Beliefs

Grounded in the empirical research, DEC's recommended practices also embrace some fundamental values that are described in this section. For additional discussion of these values and beliefs see *DEC Positions and Concept Papers*, Appendix C.

Respect for all children and families

Respect for all children and families is a fundamental value supported by DEC. All children and families means all—including children with disabilities, children at-risk for school failure, children who live in poverty, children who are non-English speaking, children with gifts and talents, and all of their families.

Respect for all children and families is a fundamental value supported by DEC.

In addition, the concept of respect for all children and families was articulated in one of our focus groups, the Cultural and Linguistic Sensitivity group. The group amplified the understanding that cultures are not static but rather are dynamic and fluid. Everyone is diverse, and we are all members of several different cultural and/or linguistic groups. The term *culture* is broadly defined to include beliefs, values, and traditions associated with race, ethnicity, language, and social and economic status.

Culture and language are integrated within each of us and within each child and family. Each individual's culture and language should be honored and acknowledged in ways that do not make them seem unusual or exotic. We need to recognize that each individual's culture and language are one of many, enabling us to be more open and accepting of various cultures and languages and to view other cultures and languages as equally valid to our own.

Differences exist among members of cultural and linguistic groups. That is, there are intragroup as well as intergroup differences. Individuals affiliate themselves with various cultural and linguistic groups. Behavior or attitude based on group affiliation should not be predicted. Barrera (2000) wrote that "The purpose of recognizing culture and cultural dynamics is not to predict or anticipate. It is, rather, to become open and respectful to diverse behaviors even when these are outside of our areas of familiarity" (p. 18).

A power differential too often exists between families and service providers. Language, race, ethnicity, educational attainment, and social and economic status influence knowledge about and access to EI/ECSE services and supports. These factors also have an impact on the way services are received.

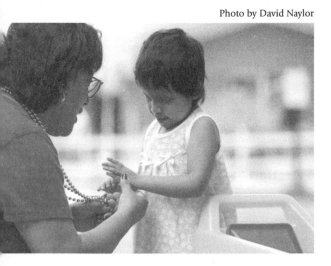

Photo by David Naylor

Each child and family's dignity and their right to privacy should be respected. It is important that we ensure that children and their families maintain their dignity and identity as they cross the bridge between the family's culture and the culture of early intervention and early childhood special education.

Finally, we must recognize that we view individuals and the world around us through "culturally-tinted lenses" (Barrera, 2000). Though professionals may share some characteristics and experiences with the children and families they serve, each of us has our own views and behaviors. Kalyanpur and Harry (1999) wrote,

there is no evidence that professionals who do belong to the same culture as their clients are any more successful at accomplishing collaborative relationships than those who do not; on the contrary, as studies (Harry, 1992; Ladson-Billings, 1994) indicated, the best examples of collaborative relationships can occur with professionals who have little or no affiliation with the culture of families. (p. 131)

High-quality, comprehensive, coordinated, and family-centered services and supports

DEC supports the identification and delivery of high quality, comprehensive, coordinated, and family-centered services and supports that help children reach their full potential. This value is based on the belief that high-quality EI/ECSE services and supports make a positive difference in the lives of young children and their families. EI/ECSE can help ensure that children attain meaningful and functional skills and that their families are supported in their role of nurturing and guiding their children.

Services and supports are individualized based on the child's strengths and needs, and on the family's priorities and concerns. Thus EI/ECSE encompasses a variety of services and supports that range in intensity, specificity, and frequency based on the child's needs rather than what is available from the program. Inasmuch as services and supports can be diverse and complex, collaboration and coordination are required to ensure that the individuals and agencies that work with or on behalf of the child and family come to agreement on goals and strategies and share scarce resources.

DEC acknowledges that the family is the constant in the child's life. This belief recognizes that practices should honor and facilitate the family's caregiving and decision-making roles. Services and supports should be delivered in a manner that conforms to the family's life style, priorities, and concerns.

Recognizing the central role of the family, all of the involved providers, agencies, and family members must work together as a team rather than as individuals. Collaboration requires shared goals, open and effective communication, and a willingness to discuss and solve problems as a team. Collaborative skills must be taught and practiced in personnel preparation programs. Further, service delivery structures must be in place that provide the time, resources, and other supports to provide EI/ECSE in a collaborative and integrated way.

Rights of all children to participate actively and meaningfully within their families and communities

DEC believes in the rights of all children, regardless of their diverse abilities, to participate actively and meaningfully within their families and communities. The principle of normalization continues to be a useful guide. Normalization has been defined as "making available to all persons with disabilities patterns of life and conditions of everyday living which are as close as possible to the regular circumstances and ways of life of society" (Nirje, 1985, p. 67). For young children, these "patterns of life and conditions of everyday living" also present prime opportunities for learning. Traditionally, intervention was delivered in a clinic or special setting with little or no interface with the family's life at home or within their community. Valuing the child's meaningful participation in family and community environments has significant implications for practice.

Young children with disabilities do not have to be in a particular place with particular materials or people in order to learn. Learning opportunities abound for children in their home and community environments. Opportunities for learning in the child's natural settings should be identified. A natural setting is one in which the child would spend time if he or she did not have a disability. But simply being in such settings is not enough. The individual learning needs of the child must be identified, and the learning opportunities that occur in those settings must also be identified. Effective, well-matched intervention strategies and supports should be identified. Families and caregivers can then use these strategies and supports to enhance natural settings as environments for learning.

Recommended Practices for All Children

Children with disabilities and other special needs are, first of all, children. When we think about practices that will help to optimize young children's development we need to look beyond the orientation of children with special needs to include a number of other guides and standards to help us provide quality services for all young children and their families. Two such guides are described here.

The National Association for the Education of Young Children (NAEYC) publishes position statements on developmentally appropriate practices for the education and care of young children (Bredekamp & Copple, 1997). It is NAEYC's aim to promote high-quality programs for all children and their families. These developmentally appropriate practices serve as the necessary foundation for quality programs for all children.

Children with disabilities and other special needs are, first of all, children.

Another important resource for informing practices for young children is the Head Start Program Performance Standards (Administration on Children, Youth, and Families, 1999). Head Start serves young children, pregnant women, and their families. Their goal is to improve outcomes for young children in low-income families. By law, at least 10% of enrollment opportunities must be available to children with disabilities. Thus Head Start represents a significant inclusion opportunity for the early education of young children with disabilities. The standards and guidance provide Head Start programs and those who collaborate with them with valuable information and support for serving children in integrated, developmentally appropriate programs.

The DEC Recommended Practices build on this foundation of quality programs for all children. The DEC practices are intended to help meet the individual and unique needs of young children with disabilities and their families.

Organization of the Book

The number and organization of the topical strands of practice as they appear in this book reflect changes in the project from its original conceptualization through identification and validation of the practices. We began the project with a view of the field of early intervention/early childhood special education as being made up of *direct services* and of *indirect supports* that are necessary for the direct services to occur. We also expected that the practices would sort into two sets according to age: an infant and toddler set, and a preschool set.

Direct services

We began the project with six categories or strands of direct service practices: child-focused interventions, family-based practices, cultural/linguistic sensitivity, interdisciplinary models, technology applications, and learning environments. It soon became apparent that we needed to add the category of assessment.

Cultural/linguistic sensitivity crossed all other categories. It also represented a fundamental value. In collaboration with the strand participants, it was decided that the practices identified by this focus group would be embedded within the other categories rather than have this category stand apart from the others. Further, these practices undergird one of our central values as discussed earlier.

Learning environments are the places where children experience learning opportunities that promote and enhance behavioral and develop-mental competencies. Members of this focus group identified many critical practices. At the synthesis phase, we recognized the consistency of practices in this strand with those in other strands. Consequently, in collaboration with the strand participants it was decided that practices related to learning environments would be embedded throughout the other categories of practices.

Thus, we have five *direct services* strands:

- Assessment
- Child-Focused Interventions
- Family-Based Practices
- Interdisciplinary Models
- Technology Applications

Indirect supports

At the beginning of the project we adopted the concept of indirect supports to be those fundamentals necessary for high-quality direct services to occur. We organized the concept of indirect supports into three groupings: policy and procedures; personnel preparation; and systems change, maintenance, and leadership climate. The scientific focus groups generated many important practices. It became clear, however, that two of our original groupings were not necessarily distinct. Thus we combined two of the strands to form the strand of "policy, procedures, and systems change".

The third original indirect support strand, personnel preparation, also presented us with an interesting challenge. In 1995, DEC, in collaboration with NAEYC and the Association of Teacher Educators (ATE), developed and validated personnel standards for the early childhood special educator. These standards represent the necessary *content (i.e., knowledge and skills)* needed by EI/ECSE personnel. These standards are found in the Supplement to Chapter 8. The same chapter contains the recommended practices for the *design and delivery* of preservice and inservice education programs for EI/ECSE personnel. These two sets of personnel practices (i.e., knowledge and skills, and design and delivery) should be used as companion pieces.

Thus, we arrived at two strands of *indirect supports*:

- Policy, Procedures, and Systems Change
- Personnel Preparation

Age grouping

While we expected that age range (i.e., birth to 3 and 3 through 5) would be an important characteristic by which to group the practices, this did not occur. Our focus groups discussed the issue of age and whether or not birth-to-3 and preschool practices should be separated. Participants noted the similarities as well as the differences between services for infants and toddlers as compared to preschool-age children. More often than not, participants concluded that recommended practices spanned both age ranges. Thus, in this book we have not separated the age groups.

Format of chapters

Each of the following seven chapters of DEC's Recommended Practices begins with an introductory statement written by the research strand chairs. Their introductions include the organizing principles or key features that serve as the foundation for each strand. Also included are definitions of terms that are specific to the strand. (A glossary of additional terms is found in Appendix D.) A listing of the recommended practices follows the introduction in each chapter. The practices are grouped under unifying statements. In Chapter 10 the reader will find applications that illustrate a few ways that the practices can be used in the field. In future products we will provide examples and other information to help implement the practices in a variety of settings.

References

Administration on Children, Youth, and Families (ACYF). (1999). *Head Start program performance standards and other regulations.* Washington, DC: Author.

Barrera, I. (2000). Honoring differences: Essential features of appropriate ECSE services for young children from diverse sociocultural environments. *Young Exceptional Children 3*(4), 17-24.

Bredekamp, S., & Copple, C. (Eds.). (1997). *Developmentally appropriate practice in early childhood programs.* Washington, DC: National Association for the Education of Young Children.

Bryant, D.M., Burchinal, M., Lau, L., & Sparling, J.J. (1994). Family and classroom correlates of Head Start children's development outcomes. *Early Childhood Research Quarterly, 9,* 289-309.

Burchinal, M.R., Lee, M., & Ramey, C. (1989). Type of day care and preschool intellectual development in disadvantaged children. *Child Development, 60,* 128-137.

Burchinal, M.R., Roberts, J.E., Nabors, L.A., & Bryant, D.M. (1996). Quality of center child care and infant cognitive and language development. *Child Development, 67,* 606-620.

Buysse, V., & Bailey, D.B. (1993). Behavioral and developmental outcomes in young children with disabilities in integrated and segregated settings: A review of comparative studies. *Journal of Special Education, 26,* 434-461.

Child Care Action Campaign. (2000, August). High-quality child care can improve children's school readiness by 50%. *ChildCare ActioNews, 17*(4), 1, 8.

Cost, Quality, and Child Outcomes Study Team. (1995). *Cost, quality, and child outcomes in child care centers public report.* Denver: University of Colorado at Denver, Economics Department.

Diamond, M., & Hopson, J. (1999). *Magic trees of the mind: How to nurture your child's intelligence, creativity, and healthy emotions from birth through adolescence.* New York: Plume.

Harry, B. (1992). Developing cultural self-awareness: The first step in values clarification for early interventionists. *Topics in Early Childhood Special Education, 12,* 333-350.

Hebbeler, K.M., Smith, B.J., & Black, T.L. (1991). Federal early childhood special education policy: A model for the improvement of services for children with disabilities. *Exceptional Children, 58,* 104-112.

Howes, C., Phillips, D.A., & Whitebook, M. (1992). Thresholds of quality: Implications for the social development of children in center-based child care. *Child Development, 63,* 449-460.

Kalyanpur, M., & Harry, B. (1999). *Culture in special education.* Baltimore: Paul H. Brookes.

Ladson-Billings, G. (1994). *The dreamkeepers: Successful teachers of African-American children.* San Francisco: Jossey-Bass.

Nirje, B. (1985). The basis and logic of the normalization principle. *Australia and New Zealand Journal of Developmental Disabilities, 11*(2), 65-68.

Shore, R. (1997). *Rethinking the brain: New insights into early development.* New York: Families and Work Institute.

Notes

Direct Services

• • • • •

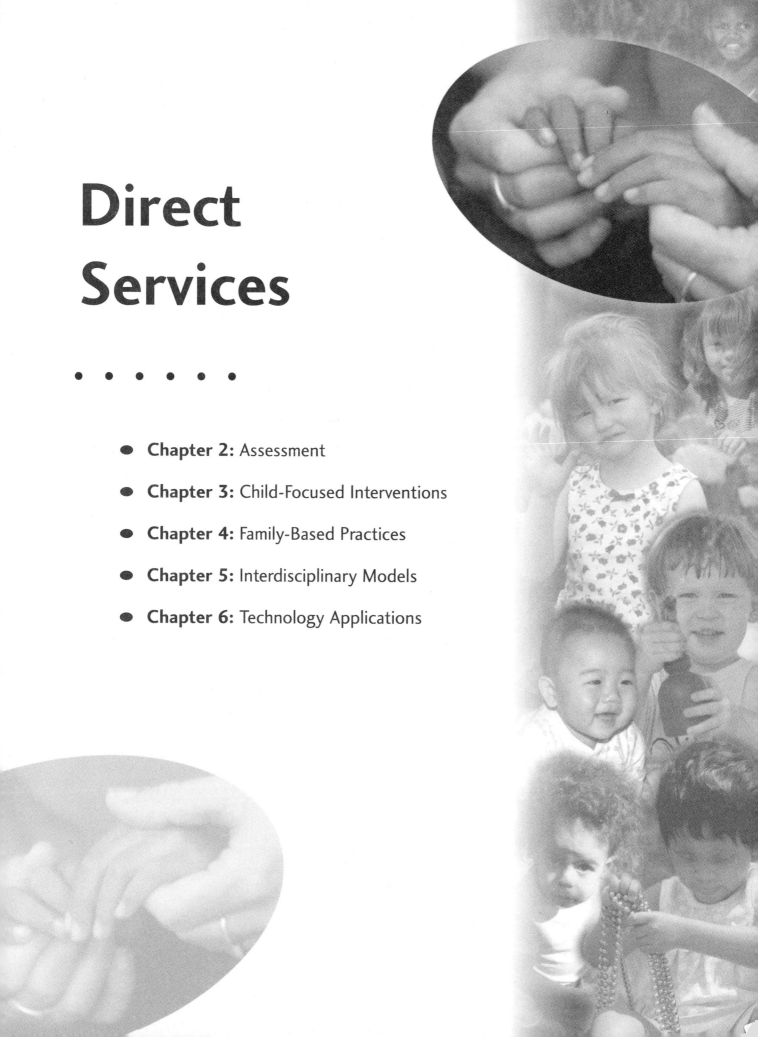

Chapter 2

Recommended Practices in Assessment

. . . .

John T. Neisworth and Stephen J. Bagnato

Professionals and families have promoted some notable changes in assessment for early intervention/early childhood special education since the early 1980s. Yet, these changes are meager in comparison to fundamental transformations witnessed in EI/ECSE: use of natural settings, developmentally appropriate practices, and family-centered methods. In this respect, assessment for early intervention has been *delayed* in its own development. Materials that are family friendly and that link assessment and teaching seem critical to early intervention; however, few changes have occurred in the process, style, and methods of assessment to complement inclusion or developmentally appropriate and family-centered practices.

Assessment is a pivotal event for families and their children; assessment results are used to include or exclude children from specialized interventions that can change their developmental destinies. Beyond the eligibility determination or *gate keeping* purpose, assessment also is critical for program planning, for monitoring (formative) progress, and for program (summative) evaluation. Given the importance of assessment, it is understandable that the materials and procedures for early childhood assessment are contentious. The professional literature, newsletters of parent organizations—and, indeed, the pages read by hearing officers—illustrate the assessment struggle.

The recommended practices included in this chapter emerged from the various focus groups and are supported with the literature. In addition, they reflect the ideas and experiences of many professionals and families with whom we have collaborated over several years. The practices also echo many of the suggestions and concerns of other professional standards, including the National Association for the Education of Young Children (NAEYC, 1991), the National Association of Early Childhood Specialists in State Departments of Education (1991), the National Association of School Psychologists (see Thomas & Grimes, 1995), the American Speech-Language-Hearing Association (1990), and the Association for Childhood Education International (ACEI—see Perrone, 1991). Previously, we proposed a definition for early childhood assessment that is consistent with the recommendations reported in this chapter.

Early childhood assessment is a flexible, collaborative decision-making process in which teams of parents and professionals repeatedly revise their judgments and reach consensus about the changing developmental, educational, medical, and mental health service needs of young children and their families. (Bagnato & Neisworth, 1991, p. xi)

Key Features

The professionals and parents who participated in this effort repeatedly expressed two concerns: First, as principal stakeholders, parents and family members must play a vital and indispensable role in assessment from beginning to end. Second, assessment methods and materials must accommodate children's developmental and disability-specific characteristics. Because of the importance of these concerns, they are presented separately.

Early childhood assessment is a flexible, collaborative decision-making process . . . .

Parents as partners

As professionals, we are committed to working with parents and others who know and care about the child. It is true, of course, that there are obstacles to effective family participation. Families may be overwhelmed by their child's possible diagnosis and can be intimidated by jargon and by differences in educational levels. Cultural differences; language barriers; and work, health, schedule, and transportation difficulties can make collaboration difficult.

In addition to our legal and ethical responsibility to partner with parents, there are sound professional and practical reasons. First, families provide valuable authentic and longitudinal information about their child that is not otherwise available (e.g., Diamond & Squires, 1993). Because of differing perspectives and contexts, professionals and families should be considered independent rather than interchangeable raters (Suen, Lu, & Neisworth, 1993). Further, family members provide needed information about their circumstances and the possible impact on the child. More active involvement of parents in their child's program appears to be related to greater developmental progress (Ramey & Ramey, 1998). Not an isolated or perfunctory recommendation, parents as partners is a dominant theme that runs across all phases of the assessment sequence.

Developmental appropriateness

Organizations representing young children (e.g., NAEYC, ACEI) have for some time advocated approaches and materials that match children's interests and developmental status. Early childhood professionals oppose the use of school-age demands and practices with children who are neither developmentally prepared for nor benefiting from such imposition. Conventional standardized norm-referenced assessment materials and tasks are very often seen as entirely wrong even for use with children of typical development (Perrone, 1991). The *inappropriateness* of such materials and demands becomes greatly exacerbated when considering young children with special needs (Bagnato, Neisworth, & Munson, 1997):

> *Assessment of infants and preschoolers remains dominated by restrictive methods and styles that place a premium on inauthentic, contrived developmental tasks, that are administered by various professionals in separate sessions using small, unmotivating toys from boxes or test kits, staged at a table or on the floor in an unnatural setting, observed passively by parents, interpreted by norms based solely on typical children, and used for narrow purposes of classification and eligibility determination.* (p. 69)

The styles, methods, and content of assessment must become compatible with, rather than at odds with, the behavior and interests of young children. A fundamental precept of developmentally appropriate practice is that teaching and assessment must take place in the child's natural context—rather than decontextualized.

> *A developmental approach presumes a more whole-child view. Many developmental areas are sampled and child differences, from time-to-time, are highlighted so that the child's previous performance serves as the baseline for monitoring progress. Professionals use a flexible approach in choosing toys that are motivating for the child and are often the child's own. They are responsive to the fact that young children rarely sit still at tables or respond on command to typical structured tasks. A developmental approach acknowledges that professionals must adjust their own language, behavior, and expectations to the young child's level of developmental maturity. A more familiar play-based approach is used that does not force conformance to standardized procedures that are at odds with the typical behavior of young children.* (Bagnato & Neisworth, 2000, p. 1)

New directions and professional standards for early childhood assessment must reflect eight critical qualities: Assessment must be useful, acceptable, authentic, collaborative, convergent, equitable, sensitive, and congruent (Bagnato & Neisworth, 1999). These eight qualities operationalize the concept of developmentally appropriate practice and parents as partners in assessment for early intervention.

Suggested Standards/Definition of Terms

Utility. Assessment must be useful to accomplish the multiple and interrelated purposes of early care and education and early intervention. Assessment is critical for detecting possible problems and, through intervention, averting later more intractable and complex difficulties. Children must be entered into programs through flexible eligibility determination processes; assessment is crucial for planning individualized interventions, for monitoring progress through regular repeated assessments, and for documenting the impact of quality programs. Above all, assessment must have treatment validity—there must be an essential similarity or linkage among program goals, individual child objectives, and the developmental competencies that are assessed.

Materials and methods of assessment should help families and professionals to identify instructional objectives and methods for helping.

Acceptability. The methods, styles, and materials for assessment must be mutually agreed upon by families and professionals. The objectives and methods suggested by assessment must be considered worthwhile and acceptable. Further, assessment should detect changes in behavior that are noticeable to caregivers in home and early childhood environments. This standard of acceptability is an aspect of the wider construct usually referred to as social validity.

Authenticity. Contrived tasks and materials as well as unfamiliar people and circumstances are not optimal for true appraisals of what children really know and do. Tabletop testing with tiny little toys is often a task dreaded by the child, parents, and, indeed, the professional!

Psychometric items typically do not sample useful curricular content that could guide intervention. Observing children performing in their natural situations offers authentic information that is much more descriptive of the child. Rating scales, direct observation, curriculum-based checklists, and caregiver interview inventories are useful in helping professionals get a realistic appraisal of the child's strengths and intervention priorities.

Collaboration. Assessment methods and styles should promote teamwork among families and professionals. Parents and other family members are central partners in the

assessment of their children; assessment materials should be chosen and used because they are written in understandable, family-friendly, jargon-free language to which anyone can respond. Assessment must promote the concept of parent-professional decision making in which "tests do not make decisions—people do." Curriculum-based assessment can be used as a unifying approach that invites input from multiple team members, including family members.

Convergence. Functional, reliable, and valid information on the status and progress of children can be obtained when typical behavior in everyday routines is observed repeatedly by several individuals—teachers, other professionals, and parents. Differences in such data are important to highlight so that areas for needed change or special emphasis in programming can be underscored. The pooling (convergence) of several perspectives (family, professional) provides a better information base.

Equity. Assessment must accommodate individual differences. The principle of equity is recognized (and mandated) as essential for instructional materials. For example, one would not use standard print material with children of low vision. Materials can be chosen that allow the child to demonstrate capabilities through several different response modes using materials that can be changed in a flexible manner. When materials and procedures accommodate a child's sensory, response, affective, and cultural characteristics, they are equitable. Conventional materials have been standardized with children of typical development; to force fit these materials on atypical children violates not only the standard of equity and developmental appropriateness, but common sense.

Sensitivity. Professionals and families must be given the opportunity to use assessment materials that sample evidence of progressively more complex skill development so that even the smallest increment of change can be detected and celebrated. Children with more severe delays and impairments especially need assessment that is sensitive to small increments of progress. Many conventional instruments do not include a sufficient number of items to make possible sensitive measurement of progress.

When materials and procedures accommodate a child's sensory, response, affective, and cultural characteristics, they are equitable.

Congruence. Materials must be designed for, and field-validated on, the very children who will be assessed, including those with typical development and those with varying degrees of mild to severe disabilities. Early intervention, specifically, and early childhood education, generally, require specialized materials that address the emerging talents of young children at play in various home and center-based educational settings. Early childhood assessment materials and methods must be developed specifically for infants and preschool children and match the style and interests typical of young children.

Organization of the Practices

A glance at the headings for the assessment recommended practices show that they are organized around five statements. These emphasize (a) professional and family collaboration, (b) individualized and appropriate assessment, (c) useful information, (d) respectful sharing of information, and (e) meeting requirements. Two central themes or dimensions inform all of the practices: (a) parents are partners in assessment, and (b) materials and practices must be developmentally appropriate.

Using This Chapter

Families as well as professionals may want to use the recommendations as a checklist to appraise personal or program assessment practices. A scoring system could be developed that records emerging practice as well as those that are well established or absent. Two or one more columns might be used to enter appraisals at two or more times, to show progress. Used in this way, the recommendations might serve as a kind of curriculum-based assessment of assessment practices. Likewise, families might use the checklist to evaluate agency/school practices. Such appraisal can be helpful to families as well as professionals who are sincerely interested in family members' perspective and evaluations.

References

American Speech-Language-Hearing Association. (1990). *Guidelines for practices in early intervention.* Rockville, MD: Author.

Bagnato, S.J., & Neisworth, J.T. (1991). *Assessment for early intervention: Best practices for professionals.* New York: Guilford.

Bagnato, S.J., & Neisworth, J.T. (1999). Collaboration and teamwork in assessment for early intervention. *Child and Adolescent Psychiatric Clinics of North America, 8*(2), 347-363.

Bagnato, S.J., & Neisworth, J.T. (2000, Spring). Assessment is adjusted to each child's developmental needs. *Birth through 5 Newsletter, 1*(2), 1.

Bagnato, S.J., Neisworth, J.T., & Munson, S.M. (1997). *LINKing: Assessment and early intervention.* Baltimore: Paul H. Brookes.

Diamond, K., & Squires, J. (1993). The role of parental report in the screening and assessment of young children. *Journal of Early Intervention, 17*(2), 107-115.

National Association for the Education of Young Children and National Association of Early Childhood Specialists in State Departments of Education. (1991). *Position statement: Guidelines for appropriate curriculum content and assessment in programs serving children ages 3 through 8* (NAEYC No. 725). Washington, DC: Author.

Perrone, V. (1991). On standardized testing. *Childhood Education,* Spring, 132-142.

Ramey, C.T., & Ramey, S.L. (1998). Early intervention and early experience. *American Psychologist, 53*(2), 109-120.

Suen, H.K., Lu, C.H., & Neisworth, J.T. (1993). Measurement of team decision-making through generalizability theory. *Journal of Psychoeducational Assessment, 11,* 120-132.

Thomas, A., & Grimes, J. (1995). *Best practices in school psychology III.* Bethesda, MD: National Association of School Psychologists.

DEC Recommended Practices: Assessment

Professionals and families collaborate in planning and implementing assessment.

. . . .

A1. Professionals provide families with easy access by phone or other means for arranging initial screening and other activities.

. . . .

A2. Professionals ensure a single point of contact for families throughout the assessment process.

. . . .

A3. Families receive a written statement of program philosophy regarding family participation in assessment planning and activities.

. . . .

A4. Professionals meet and collaborate with families to discuss family preferences and reach consensus about the process, methods, materials, and situations of assessment that will meet the child's needs best.

. . . .

A5. Professionals solicit information from families regarding the child's interests, abilities, and special needs.

. . . .

A6. Professionals review, with parental consent, agency information about the child and family.

. . . .

A7. Professionals and families identify team members and the team assessment style to fit best the needs and goals of the child and family.

. . . .

A8. Families participate actively in assessment procedures.

. . . .

A9. Families choose their roles in the assessment of their children (e.g., assistant, facilitator, observer, assessor).

. . . .

A10. With each family's agreement, professionals help families identify their resources, concerns and priorities related to their child's development.

A11. Professionals, families, and other regular caregivers work as equal team members for purposes of assessment (i.e., give equal priority to family/caregiver's observations and reports, discuss assessment results, reach consensus about the child's needs and programs).

A12. Program administrators encourage the use of assessment procedures that ensure consultation and collaboration among families and professionals (e.g., the whole team discusses qualitative and quantitative information and negotiate consensus to make decisions).

Assessment is individualized and appropriate for the child and family.

A13. Professionals use multiple measures to assess child status, progress, and program impact and outcomes (e.g., developmental observations, criterion/curriculum-based, interviews, informed clinical opinion, and curriculum-compatible norm-referenced scales).

A14. Professionals choose materials and procedures that accommodate the child's sensory, physical, responsive, and temperamental differences.

A15. Professionals rely on materials that capture the child's authentic behaviors in routine circumstances.

A16. Professionals seek information directly from families and other regular caregivers using materials and procedures that the families themselves can manage to design IFSP/IEP goals and activities.

A17. Professionals assess children in contexts that are familiar to the child.

A18. Professionals assess children after they have become familiar to the child.

A19. Professionals gather information from multiple sources (e.g., families, professional team members, agencies, service providers, other regular caregivers).

A20. Professionals assess the child's strengths and needs across all developmental and behavioral dimensions.

Assessment provides useful information for intervention.

....

A21. Families and professionals assess the presence and extent of atypical child behavior that may be a barrier to intervention and progress.

....

A22. Professionals use functional analysis of behavior to assess the form and function of challenging behaviors.

....

A23. Program supervisors, in concert with the EI/ECSE team, use only those measures that have high treatment validity (i.e., that link assessment, individual program planning, and progress evaluation).

....

A24. Professionals assess not only immediate mastery of a skill, but also whether the child can demonstrate the skill consistently across other settings and with other people.

....

A25. Professionals appraise the level of support that a child requires in order to perform a task.

....

A26. Professionals choose and use scales with sufficient item density to detect even small increments of progress (especially important for children with more severe disabilities).

....

A27. Professionals and families rely on curriculum-based assessment as the foundation or "mutual language" for team assessments.

....

A28. Professionals conduct longitudinal, repeated assessments in order to examine previous assumptions about the child, and to modify the ongoing program.

....

A29. Professionals report assessment results in a manner that is immediately useful for planning program goals and objectives.

Professionals share information in respectful and useful ways.

. . . .

A30. Professionals report assessment results so that they are understandable and useful for families.

. . . .

A31. Professionals report strengths as well as priorities for promoting optimal development.

. . . .

A32. Professionals report limitations of assessments (e.g., questions of rapport, cultural bias, and sensory/response requirements).

. . . .

A33. Professionals write reports that contain findings and interpretations regarding the interrelatedness of developmental areas (e.g., how the child's limitations have affected development; how the child has learned to compensate).

. . . .

A34. Professionals organize reports by developmental/functional domains or concerns rather than by assessment device.

. . . .

A35. Families have adequate time to review reports, ask questions, or express concerns before the team uses the information for decision making.

. . . .

A36. Family members may invite other individuals to evaluation meetings or meetings to discuss children's performance or progress.

Professionals meet legal and procedural requirements <u>and</u> meet recommended practice guidelines.

. . . .

A37. Professionals inform families about state EI/ECSE rules and regulations regarding assessment.

. . . .

A38. Professionals, when required by regulations to apply a diagnosis, employ measures and classification systems that are designed and developmentally appropriate for infants and young children.

. . . .

A39. Psychologists rely on authentic measures of early problem-solving skills (instead of traditional intelligence tests) that link directly to program content and goals and that sample skills in natural, rather than contrived, circumstances (e.g., play-based).

. . . .

A40. Professionals, when appropriate, choose only those norm-referenced measures that are developed, field-validated, standardized, and normed with children similar to the child being assessed.

. . . .

A41. Professionals monitor child progress based on past performance as the referent rather than on group norms.

. . . .

A42. Professionals defer a definitive diagnosis until evaluation of the child's response to a tailored set of interventions.

. . . .

A43. Program administrators provide supervisory support for team members to enable them to maintain ethical standards and recommended practices.

. . . .

A44. Professionals and families conduct an ongoing (formative) review of the child's progress at least every 90 days in order to modify instructional and therapeutic strategies.

. . . .

A45. Professionals and families assess and redesign outcomes to meet the ever changing needs of the child and family.

. . . .

A46. Professionals and families assess the child's progress on a yearly (summative) basis to modify the child's goal-plan.

Notes

Chapter 3

Recommended Practices in Child-Focused Interventions

· · · · · · · · · · · · ·

Mark Wolery

Child-focused interventions include the decisions and practices used to structure and provide learning opportunities for children. These decisions and practices include how children are taught (i.e., the strategies and practices used to ensure learning), when and where the instructional practices and arrangements are implemented, and how children's performance is monitored to make decisions about modifying the interventions and identification of other goals.

Key Features
· · · · · · · · · · · · · · · ·

This chapter is based on three straightforward assumptions. First, *a primary function of early intervention (EI) and early childhood special education (ECSE) is to promote children's learning and development* (Bailey & Wolery, 1992; Shonkoff & Meisels, 2000; Widerstrom, Mowder, & Sandall, 1997). In short, children should learn important skills and have more advanced developmental abilities as a result of participating in EI/ECSE. Clearly, EI/ECSE has other functions, but a major purpose of specialized services is to influence children's learning and developmental trajectories. This chapter focuses directly on the recommended practices for organizing and implementing such influences.

Second, *children's experiences of interacting with the social and physical environment have a primary influence on their learning and development* (Horowitz & Haritos, 1998). Other forces such as children's health and their genetic inheritance also are important influences, but children's experiences are critical. Children's experiences, of course, can have

---

Focus group members: Lise Fox, Howard Goldstein, Louise Kaczmarek, Diane Sainato, and Susan Sandall

a range of influences. Some experiences can assist them in learning desirable skills and patterns (styles) of interacting with the world, other experiences can result in little apparent learning, and still others can help them learn undesirable skills and patterns. Experiences that enhance learning or impede learning can and do occur anywhere at any time. Facilitative experiences are not restricted to children's contacts with intervention professionals or intervention programs; they occur throughout the child's day wherever the child is (McWilliam, Wolery, & Odom, in press). The tasks of early intervention professionals are (a) to maximize the likelihood that all of children's experiences, whenever and wherever they occur, will promote learning of desired skills and patterns and (b) to minimize the likelihood that children will have interactions that impede learning of desirable skills and patterns. The recommended practices in this chapter describe strategies and approaches for accomplishing these tasks; however, unthoughtful and unsystematic use of these practices will not ensure that children's experiences promote desirable learning. Thus, planful, purposeful, and careful use of the recommended practices are critical in influencing children's interactions with the world and thus their learning and development. In making this statement, however, an important qualification must be noted; specifically, not all of children's interactions with the world must be planned by professionals.

Photo by David Naylor

Clearly, many parents provide their children with an array of experiences in the home (e.g., games they play at bath time, family routines, eating with the family) and community (e.g., participating in events such as going shopping, attending religious services, going to story hour at the library) that promote learning of desirable skills. Professionals must be sure not to impose interventions that actually interfere with such events.

Third, *the field now has a good deal of research for guiding practitioners' decisions related to organizing and influencing children's experiences* (Barnett, Bell, & Carey, 1999; Guralnick, 1997; Kozloff, 1994; Odom & McLean, 1996; Shonkoff & Meisels, 2000). This research often has been conducted in service programs addressing desired skills of real children. Further, much of this research was conducted with valid measures and rigorous procedures. As a result, the field has a solid foundation from which to derive recommended practices. The existence of this research foundation means practitioners' decisions and work should not be based solely on their experiences and beliefs; rather, clear guidance is available from the literature for making many critical decisions and for using particular practices.

Organization of the Practices

Using this research base, this chapter contains recommended practices for influencing children's ongoing interactions with the social and physical world to ensure that they have experiences that will enhance their learning of desirable skills and styles of interacting. In this chapter, the recommended practices are organized by three major *take-home* messages:

1. Adults design environments to promote children's safety, active engagement, learning, participation, and membership.
2. Adults individualize and adapt practices for each child based on ongoing data to meet children's changing needs.
3. Adults use systematic procedures within and across environments, activities, and routines to promote children's learning and participation.

These messages carry some specific implications that deserve explicit note. Each message specifies that the adults do specific things (design environments, individualize and adapt practices, and use systematic procedures) in very purposeful ways to produce specific outcomes. Child-focused intervention is an intentional act on the part of the adults who care for and interact with children. Implementing child-focused intervention involves each of these functions. But designing environments is not enough; individualization and use of specific procedures must also occur. Likewise, individualizing or using specific procedures is not adequate if the children's environments have not been designed. Individualization that ignores the use of specific procedures may not work. Thus, each of these three messages contains recommendations that if used in isolation, are not adequate for providing high-quality intervention; the recommendations must be applied as a set. Doing child-focused interventions is a complex process; it is demanding; and it requires careful attention to many different issues. These three take-home messages are useful ways of organizing and thinking about this difficult task for designing interventions, for solving problems, for improving services, and for ensuring that goals are achieved. Although the recommendations that are listed under each message are based on research, solid theoretical foundations, experience, and the judgments of knowledgeable experts support these recommendations.

Child-focused intervention is an intentional act on the part of the adults who care for and interact with children.

chapter 3

Definition of Terms

Adults. In the recommended practices, the term *adults* is used several times. This term should be defined broadly to include all of the persons who are responsible for caring for, educating, or providing therapy to the young child with disabilities. As such, it includes parents, teachers, therapists, and other caregivers. It includes all of these

chapter 3

various adults because of the assumption that all of the child's interactions with the environment are potentially beneficial or harmful to the child's learning and development.

Interventionist. The term *interventionist* is used to refer specifically to the professionals (teachers, therapists, etc.) who are responsible for planning and carrying out a child's individualized EI/ECSE program.

Strategies. A strategy is an organized procedure for guiding adults' behavior in interacting with, and promoting the learning of, young children with disabilities. Such strategies have conceptual and research foundations; however, those that are listed should not be seen as the sum total of what is possible. Other strategies can be devised, and individualized strategies not listed here could be used and evaluated with individual children to address specific goals. Strategies are different from practices in that they are more specific about what adults are to do and are applied for addressing specific goals of individual children. More detailed descriptions of the strategies will be provided in future DEC products. Descriptions can be found in several of the sources in the reference list.

Using This Chapter

Despite the comprehensive nature of the recommended practices in this chapter, they do not address some critical issues related to applying child-focused interventions. These practices do not describe in detail the practices that should be used in assessing children and their environments to identify goals and plan the implementation of individualized intervention strategies (McLean, Bailey, & Wolery, 1996). This information is critical, because it helps ensure that the practices included here are not misapplied; recommended practices for conducting such assessments are found in Chapter 2. Further, this chapter does not include information on how to assist families in supporting their children's experiences (Dunst, Trivette, & Deal, 1994). When attempting to ensure that children's experiences promote learning of desired goals, there is a danger of placing expectations on parents to assume narrow roles similar to those of teachers. While parents clearly and appropriately teach their children many things, the emphasis should be on ensuring that families live normalized lives while having positive interactions between themselves and their children and providing experiences that have enhancing effects. Recommended practices for supporting and assisting families are presented in Chapter 4. This chapter also does not include information on how to work with other adults (e.g., child care staff, therapists, community play group staff) to promote children's learning and development (Bruder, 1994). Nonetheless, working effectively with such individuals is central to promoting children's learning

. . . the emphasis should be on ensuring that families live normalized lives while having positive interactions between themselves and their children . . . .

through their ongoing experiences. The chapter also does not describe practices related to the delivery of specialized therapies or tell how those specialized therapies are embedded into children's ongoing experiences (McWilliam, 1996). Recommended practices for working with other adults and implementing specialized therapies are found in Chapters 5 and 7. Finally, this chapter does not provide guidance related to placement decisions. The recommendations in this chapter assume such decisions have been made carefully; it does provide guidance, however, on how any placement should be organized and operated.

The practices in this chapter will guide adults in planning and implementing effective child-focused interventions that enhance children's learning and development. The practices can be used in conjunction with the others in the book to guide program development and improvement.

References

Bailey, D.B., & Wolery, M. (1992). *Teaching infants and preschoolers with disabilities* (2nd ed.). Columbus, OH: Macmillan.

Barnett, D.W., Bell, S.H., & Carey, K.T. (1999). *Designing preschool interventions: A practitioner's guide.* New York: Guilford.

Bruder, M.B. (1994). Working with members of other disciplines: Collaboration for success. In M. Wolery, & J.S. Wilbers (Eds.), *Including children with special needs in early childhood programs* (pp. 45-70). Washington, DC: National Association for the Education of Young Children.

Dunst, C.J., Trivette, C.M., & Deal, A.G. (1994). *Supporting and strengthening families: Vol. 1: Methods, strategies and practices.* Cambridge, MA: Brookline Books.

Guralnick, M.J. (1997). *The effectiveness of early intervention.* Baltimore: Paul H. Brookes.

Horowitz, F.D., & Haritos, C. (1998). The organism and the environment: Implications for understanding mental retardation. In J.A. Burack, R.M. Hodapp, & E. Zigler (Eds.), *Handbook of mental retardation and development* (pp. 20-40). New York: Cambridge University Press.

Kozloff, M.A. (1994). *Improving educational outcomes for children with disabilities: Principles of assessment, program planning, and evaluation.* Baltimore: Paul H. Brookes.

McLean, M., Bailey, D.B., & Wolery, M. (Eds.). (1996). *Assessing infants and preschoolers with special needs* (2nd ed.). Columbus, OH: Merrill/Prentice Hall.

McWilliam, R.A. (1996). *Rethinking pull-out services in early intervention: A professional resource.* Baltimore: Paul H. Brookes.

McWilliam, R.A., Wolery, M., & Odom, S.L. (in press). Instructional perspectives in inclusive preschool classrooms. In M. J. Guralnick (Ed.), *Early childhood inclusion: Focus on change.* Baltimore: Paul H. Brookes.

Odom, S.L., & McLean, M.E. (Eds.). (1996). *Early intervention/early childhood special education: Recommended practices.* Austin, TX: PRO-ED.

Shonkoff, J.P., & Meisels, S.J. (2000). *Handbook of early childhood intervention* (2nd ed.). Cambridge, UK: Cambridge University Press.

Widerstrom, A.H., Mowder, B.A., & Sandall, S.A. (1997). *Infant development and risk* (2nd ed.). Baltimore: Paul H. Brookes.

DEC Recommended Practices: Child-Focused Interventions

Adults design environments to promote children's safety, active engagement, learning, participation, and membership.

C1. Physical space and materials are structured and adapted to promote engagement, play, interaction, and learning by attending to children's preferences and interests, using novelty, using responsive toys, providing adequate amounts of materials, and using defined spaces.

C2. The social dimension of the environment is structured and adapted to promote engagement, interaction, communication, and learning by providing peer models, peer proximity, responsive adults, and imitative adults; and by expanding children's play and behavior.

C3. Routines and transitions are structured to promote interaction, communication, and learning by being responsive to child behavior and using naturalistic time delay, interrupted chain procedure, transition-based teaching, and visual cue systems.

C4. Play routines are structured to promote interaction, communication, and learning by defining roles for dramatic play, prompting engagement, prompting group friendship activities, and using specialized props.

C5. Environments are designed and activities are conducted so that children learn or are exposed to multiple cultures and languages by, among other practices, allowing children and families to share their cultures and languages with others, to the extent they desire.

C6. Learning environments meet accepted standards of quality including curriculum, child-staff ratios, group size, and physical design of classroom.

C7. Interventionists ensure the physical and emotional safety and security of children while children are in their care.

C8. A variety of appropriate settings and naturally occurring activities are used to facilitate children's learning and development.

C9. Services are provided in natural learning environments as appropriate. These include places in which typical children participate, such as the home or community settings.

C10. Interventionists facilitate children's engagement with their environment to encourage child-initiated learning that is not dependent on the adult's presence.

C11. Environments are provided that foster positive relationships, including peer-peer, parent/caregiver-child, and parent-caregiver relationships.

Adults individualize and adapt practices for each child based on ongoing data to meet children's changing needs.

C12. Practices are individualized for each child based on: (a) the child's current behavior and abilities across relevant domains instead of the child's diagnostic classification; (b) the family's views of what the child needs to learn; (c) interventionists' and specialists' views of what the child needs to learn; and (d) the demands, expectations, and requirements of the child's current environments. The practices as well as the goals are individualized.

C13. Practices target meaningful outcomes for the child that build upon the child's current skills and behavior and promote membership with others.

C14. Data-based decisions are used to make modifications in the practices. Child performance is monitored and data are collected to determine the impact of the practices on the child's progress, and the monitoring must be feasible and useful within the child's environments (i.e., ongoing monitoring must be user friendly) and is used to make modifications of intervention if needed.

C15. Recommended practices are used to teach/promote whatever skills are necessary for children to function more completely, competently, adaptively, and independently in the child's natural environment. These skills should include teaching those that maximize participation and membership in home, school, and community environments—including those that are typical or similar to other persons' in that environment. Attention should be given to the breadth and sophistication of the child's skills. Examples of important skills across many children are

chapter
3

- being actively engaged with materials, objects, activities, and other people (peers and adults)
- being an initiator (i.e., child initiates play, social interactions, communicative exchanges, etc. without assistance from adults)
- being responsive to the initiations and behavior of others, including peers and adults
- reading the cues of the environment and responding appropriately based on those cues without being directed by adults
- having social interactions and relationships with family, peers, and others
- communicating with others, including peers and adults

C16. Children's behavior is recognized, interpreted in context, and responded to contingently, and opportunities are provided for expansion or elaboration of child behavior by imitating the behavior, waiting for the child's responses, modeling, and prompting.

Adults use systematic procedures within and across environments, activities, and routines to promote children's learning and participation.

C17. Interventionists are agents of change to promote and accelerate learning, and that learning should be viewed in different phases that require different types of practices. Phases are
- acquisition—learning how to do the skill
- fluency—learning to do the skill smoothly and at natural rates
- maintenance—learning to do the skill after instruction has stopped, and
- generalization—learning to apply the skill whenever and wherever it is needed.

C18. Practices are used systematically, frequently, and consistently within and across environments (e.g., home, center, community) and across people (i.e., those who care for and interact regularly with the child).

C19. Planning occurs prior to implementation, and that planning considers the situation (home, classroom, etc.) to which the interventions will be applied.

C20. Practices are used that are validated, normalized, useful across environments, respectful, and not stigmatizing of the child and family and that are sensitive to cultural and linguistic issues.

C21. Consequences for children's behavior are structured to increase the complexity and duration of children's play, engagement, appropriate behavior, and learning by using differential reinforcement, response shaping, high-probability procedures (i.e., behavioral momentum), and correspondence training.

C22. Systematic naturalistic teaching procedures such as models, expansions, incidental teaching, mand-model procedure, and naturalistic time delay are used to promote acquisition and use of communication and social skills.

C23. Peer-mediated strategies are used to promote social and communicative behavior.

C24. Prompting and prompt fading procedures (e.g., modeling, graduated guidance, increasing assistance, time delay) are used to ensure acquisition and use of communicative, self-care, cognitive, and social skills.

C25. Specialized procedures (e.g., naturalistic strategies and prompt/prompt fading strategies) are embedded and distributed within and across activities.

C26. Recommended instructional strategies are used with sufficient fidelity, consistency, frequency, and intensity to ensure high levels of behavior occurring frequently.

C27. For problem behaviors, interventionists assess the behavior in context to identify its function, and then devise interventions that are comprehensive in that they make the behavior irrelevant (child's environment is modified so that problem behavior is unnecessary or precluded), inefficient (a more efficient replacement behavior is taught), and ineffective (i.e., reinforcement and other consequent events are used).

Notes

Chapter 4

Recommended Practices in Family-Based Practices

· · · · · · · · · · · ·

Carol M. Trivette and Carl J. Dunst

Photo by David Naylor

There has been considerable discussion among early intervention and early childhood special education professionals regarding what are best practices when working with families of young children with developmental disabilities or who are at risk for developmental delays. Our involvement with the DEC recommended practices project began by convening a focus group of DEC members to discuss the research evidence suggesting the types of practices that are most likely to have a positive impact on families and their abilities to care for their children. The outcome of this discussion was a definition and a set of family-based practices. The practices that were discussed resulted in the following statement regarding the parameters of family-based practices:

> *Family-based practices provide or mediate the provision of resources and supports necessary for families to have the time, energy, knowledge, and skills to provide their children learning opportunities and experiences that promote child development. Resources and supports provided as part of early intervention/early childhood special education (EI/ECSE) are done in a family-centered manner so family-based practices will have child, parent, and family strengthening and competency-enhancing consequences.*

Two aspects of this definition of family-based practices are important to underscore. The first relates to the nature of the resources and supports that are considered important for improving family functioning. A broad-based view of resources and supports is suggested, including a variety of types of informal and formal supports or resources needed by family members to promote their child's development. The second aspect of these practices is the focus on how and in what manner supports and resources are provided in order to enhance the competency of parents and strengthen the family.

Focus group members: Harriet Boone, Barbara Bowman, Carl J. Dunst, Marilyn Espe-Sherwindt, Richard Roberts, and Carol M. Trivette

Key Features

Resources and supports

According to Bronfenbrenner (1979), families need both informal and formal resources and supports so that they have both the knowledge and skills, and the time and energy to promote the development of their children. Research evidence now indicates that social support has positive effects on parental well-being, that parental sense of well-being is directly related to responsive styles of interaction, and that both responsiveness and facilitation styles of interaction are related to child development. For example, Dunst (1999) reported findings demonstrating the direct and indirect influences of social support as well as family socioeconomic status (SES) on parent well-being and parent interactional style, and the positive influence of highly supportive and minimally directive parenting styles on child development.

The model shown in Figure 1 depicts the direct and indirect influences of social support on personal and family well-being, parent-child interactions, and child behavior and development that are now supported by research findings (Dunst, 1999; Trivette, Dunst, & Hamby, 1996). According to this model, social support and resources directly influence the health and well-being of parents; both support and health/well being influence parenting styles; and support, well-being, and parenting styles directly and indirectly influence child behavior and development (Dunst, 1999, 2000; Trivette, Deal, & Dunst, 1986). Providing or mediating the supports that parents need ensures that they have the resources necessary to have the time and both the physical and psychological energy to engage in child rearing responsibilities and parenting activities (Bronfenbrenner, 1979).

Research evidence now indicates that social support has positive effects on parental well-being . . . .

Figure 1. Model depicting the direct and indirect influences of social support and intrafamily factors on parents and family well-being, parenting styles, and child behavior and development.

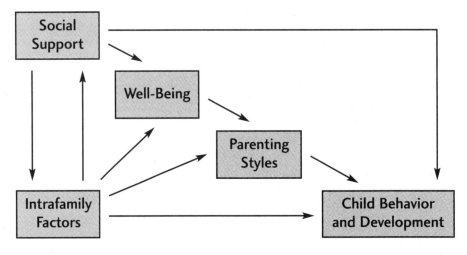

Family-centered helpgiving

The second key feature of family-based practices concerns the manner in which the resources and supports are provided to parents and families. There is now considerable agreement and understanding about the fact that *how* interventions are done matters as much as *what* is done if helpgiving is to have positive effects on families and young children (Brickman et al., 1983; Dunst & Trivette, 1988; Dunst, Trivette, Gordon, & Starnes, 1993; Karuza & Rabinowitz, 1986; Rappaport, 1981). The effects of how something is done beyond the effects of what is done are referred to as value-added benefits (Dunst & Trivette, 1996).

Research indicates that when more family-centered practices are used in working with families, there are more positive consequences in terms of families valuing the support and help they receive from early intervention providers (Dunst, Brookfield, & Epstein, 1998). A number of recent studies have used structural equation modeling (Bentler, 1995) to demonstrate the important mediating effects of family-centered helpgiving on a number of parent, family, and child outcome measures (Dunst, 2000; Dunst et al., 1993; King, Rosenbaum, & King, 1997; Thompson et al., 1997).

The provision of resources and supports to parents and families that enables them to promote the development of their children is one aspect of the family-based practices. The value-added effect of using practices that strengthen the competency of families while providing them support and resources is the other focus of these family-based practices. Professionals must strengthen families' abilities to support the development of their children, in a manner that increases families' sense of parenting competence and not families' sense of dependency on professionals or professional systems.

Organization of the Practices

Seventeen family-based practices were identified as a result of the work conducted in this strand. The individual practices were organized into four categories or *take-home* messages around the major themes found in the practices. The four themes are (a) shared responsibility and collaboration, (b) strengthening family functioning, (c) individualized and flexible practices, and (d) strengths- and asset-based practices.

Families and professionals share responsibility and work collaboratively

The focus of the practices in this category are the types of interactions between families and professionals that promote working together to achieve goals and outcomes, as opposed to the individual actions of one party. The attainment of these outcomes occurs when both individuals share relevant information on a regular basis while identifying and achieving outcomes. To ensure full collaboration, professionals have a significant responsibility to share all information in a way that matches the family's style of understanding and processing information.

Practices strengthen family functioning

These practices promote a way of working with families that provides supports and resources that develop and strengthen families' sense of parenting competence and confidence, and other aspects of positive parent and family functioning. The practices reflect the importance of informal supports and natural community life by suggesting that early intervention and early childhood special education practices should strengthen these important aspects of families' lives. Practices should operate in ways that enhance the families' abilities to have time for a family life, including time for extended family and friends.

Practices are individualized and flexible

The essence of these practices is the understanding that families as well as the individual family members may have diverse backgrounds, beliefs, and opinions about what

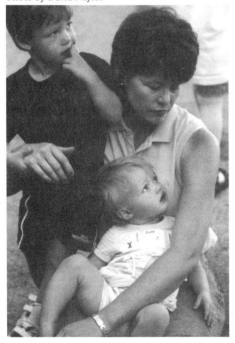

Photo by David Naylor

is important and how intervention activities should be implemented. Specific interventions must be derived from an understanding of what each family or family member wants for the child. Therefore intervention practices must be individualized to the specific family and situation. The practices in this area indicate that practitioners must be careful in making assumptions that families have beliefs and values similar to other families or to professionals. Further, the practices need to be provided in ways that minimize stress. Practitioners must examine with each individual family the family's wishes, desires, beliefs, and concerns, allowing these to determine what and how interventions are provided to both the child and the family.

Practices are strengths- and assets-based

This set of practices emphasizes that interventions must be based on the strengths and assets of children, parents, and the family in order to have the best possible outcomes. Assets are the abilities, talents, strengths, interests, capabilities, preferences, gifts, aspirations, competencies, dreams, and so forth of people . . . (Dunst & Trivette, 1996). Effective practices move beyond simply identifying the strengths and assets of children and families to using these strengths and assets as the building blocks for new information and for all interventions. For example, building participation in an activity around a child's enjoyment of music is an example of building on a child's asset. Interventions that use the strengths and assets of the family and children are more likely to have positive competency-enhancing outcomes.

Using This Chapter

This chapter will be helpful to readers in two ways. First, professionals and other care-givers now have a set of clearly defined practices regarding the types of interactions with families that have positive outcomes for children and families. These practices reflect a body of literature that comes from a number of professionals in the field of early intervention and early childhood special education and are, therefore, not the advice of only one group of persons. The second way these practices can be helpful to practitioners is by providing a framework for reflecting on their personal practices. By organizing the practices in four major themes we hope to provide professionals with direction in order to focus their understanding of the important aspects of working with families. For professionals who want to reflect on their practices with families to determine how to improve their skills, the four themes will center their efforts. Professionals will now know what is considered important when supporting families, and will have a way of thinking about these practices that allows for personal reflection and growth.

Professionals will now know what is considered important when supporting families . . . .

References

Bentler, P. (1995). *EQS structural equation modeling manual.* Encino, CA: Multivariate Software.

Brickman, P., Kidder, L.H., Coates, D., Rabinowitz, V., Cohn, E., & Karuza, J. (1983). The dilemmas of helping: Making aid fair and effective. In J.D. Fisher, A. Nadler, & B.M. DePaulo (Eds.), *New directions in helping: Vol. 1. Recipient reactions to aid* (pp. 18-51). New York: Academic Press.

Bronfenbrenner, U. (1979). *The ecology of human development: Experiments by nature and design.* Cambridge, MA: Harvard University Press.

Dunst, C.J. (1999). Placing parent education in conceptual and empirical context. *Topics in Early Childhood Special Education, 19,* 141-147.

Dunst, C.J. (2000). Revisiting "rethinking early intervention." *Topics in Early Childhood Special Education, 20,* 96-104.

Dunst, C.J., Brookfield, J., & Epstein, J. (1998, December). *Family-centered early intervention and child, parent and family benefits: Final report.* Asheville, NC: Orelena Hawks Puckett Institute.

Dunst, C.J., & Trivette, C.M. (1988). Helping, helplessness, and harm. In J.C. Witt, S.N. Elliott, & F.M. Gresham (Eds.), *Handbook of behavior therapy in education* (pp. 343-376). New York: Plenum Press.

Dunst, C.J., & Trivette, C.M. (1996). Empowerment, effective helpgiving practices, and family-centered care. *Pediatric Nursing, 22,* 334-337, 343.

Dunst, C.J., Trivette, C.M., Gordon, N.J., & Starnes, A. L. (1993). Family-centered case management practices: Characteristics and consequences. In G.H. Singer & L.L. Powers (Eds.), *Families, disability, and empowerment: Active coping skills and strategies for family interventions* (pp. 89-118). Baltimore: Paul H. Brookes.

Karuza, J., & Rabinowitz, V. (1986). Implications of control and responsibility on helping the aged. In M. Baltes & P. Baltes (Eds.), *The psychology of control and aging* (pp. 373-396). Hillsdale, NJ: Erlbaum Associates.

King, G.A., Rosenbaum, P.L., & King, S.M. (1997). Evaluating family-centered service using a measure of parents' perceptions. *Child: Care, Health and Development, 23*(1), 47-62.

Rappaport, J. (1981). In praise of paradox: A social policy of empowerment over prevention. *American Journal of Community Psychology, 9,* 1-25.

Thompson, L., Lobb, C., Elling, R., Herman, S., Jurkiewicz, T., & Hulleza, C. (1997). Pathways to family empowerment: Effects of family-centered delivery of early intervention services. *Exceptional Children, 64*(1), 99-113.

Trivette, C.M., Deal, A., & Dunst, C.J. (1986). Family needs, sources of support and professional roles: Critical elements of family systems assessment and intervention. *Diagnostique, 11,* 246-267.

Trivette, C.M., Dunst, C.J., & Hamby, D.W. (1996). Social support and coping in families of children at risk for developmental disabilities. In M. Brambring, H. Raub, & A. Beelman (Eds.), *Early childhood intervention: Theory, evaluation and practice* (pp. 234-264). Berlin, Germany: de Gruyter.

DEC Recommended Practices: Family-Based Practices

Families and professionals share responsibility and work collaboratively.

. . . .

F1. Family members and professionals jointly develop appropriate family-identified outcomes.

. . . .

F2. Family members and professionals work together and share information routinely and collaboratively to achieve family-identified outcomes.

. . . .

F3. Professionals fully and appropriately provide relevant information so parents can make informed choices and decisions.

. . . .

F4. Professionals use helping styles that promote shared family/professional responsibility in achieving family-identified outcomes.

. . . .

F5. Family/professionals' relationship building is accomplished in ways that are responsive to cultural, language, and other family characteristics.

Practices strengthen family functioning.

. . . .

F6. Practices, supports, and resources provide families with participatory experiences and opportunities promoting choice and decision making.

. . . .

F7. Practices, supports, and resources support family participation in obtaining desired resources and supports to strengthen parenting competence and confidence.

. . . .

F8. Intrafamily, informal, community, and formal supports and resources (e.g., respite care) are used to achieve desired outcomes.

. . . .

F9. Supports and resources provide families with information, competency-enhancing experiences, and participatory opportunities to strengthen family functioning and promote parenting knowledge and skills.

F10. Supports and resources are mobilized in ways that are supportive and do not disrupt family and community life.

Practices are individualized and flexible.

F11. Resources and supports are provided in ways that are flexible, individualized, and tailored to the child's and family's preferences and styles, and promote well-being.

F12. Resources and supports match each family member's identified priorities and preferences (e.g., mother's and father's may be different).

F13. Practices, supports, and resources are responsive to the cultural, ethnic, racial, language, and socioeconomic characteristics and preferences of families and their communities.

F14. Practices, supports, and resources incorporate family beliefs and values into decisions, intervention plans, and resources and support mobilization.

Practices are strengths- and assets-based.

F15. Family and child strengths and assets are used as a basis for engaging families in participatory experiences supporting parenting competence and confidence.

F16. Practices, supports, and resources build on existing parenting competence and confidence.

F17. Practices, supports, and resources promote the family's and professional's acquisition of new knowledge and skills to strengthen competence and confidence.

Chapter 5

Recommended Practices in Interdisciplinary Models

· · · · · · · · · · · ·

R. A. McWilliam

Professionals from multiple disciplines provide services for children birth to 5 and their families. This strand focuses on *consultative practices* from the four major specialized disciplines in EI/ECSE: early childhood special education, occupational therapy, physical therapy, and speech-language pathology (i.e., the numerous other specializations will not be emphasized, but practices might be applicable to them). Models for delivering both *home-based* and *classroom-based* (e.g., child care programs, preschools) service delivery are addressed. These models exist on continua from segregated and multidisciplinary services to integrated and transdisciplinary services. Practices for adult consumers of specialized services (e.g., family members, early childhood professionals) are incorporated into this strand.

IDEA requires some level of interdisciplinary teamwork. In both infant-toddler and preschool services, individuals from different disciplines are involved not only in assessment but in service delivery. In infant-toddler services, states must provide multiple services, many of which are carried out by specialists: home visits, special instruction, speech-language pathology and audiology, occupational therapy, physical therapy, psychological services, service coordination, medical services, screening and assessment, health services, social work, vision services, assistive technology, and transportation. In preschool services, individuals from these disciplines might be involved with an individual child, but the most common interdisciplinary challenges are among therapists (occupational, physical, speech-language) and educators (regular, special). Even before the passage of the original early intervention law (PL 99-457), researchers, practitioners, and university faculty members were paying attention to the importance of inclusion (e.g., Stoneman, Cantrell, & Hoover-Dempsey, 1983). This alerted the field that collaboration between specialists (e.g., early childhood special educators, psychologists,

Focus group members: Mary Beth Bruder, Pip Campbell, Eva Horn, Leslie Jackson, Louise Kaczmarek, Gerry Mahoney, R.A. McWilliam, and Mark Wolery

therapists) and generalists (classroom teachers, teachers' assistants, family members) was complex and necessary.

The practices within this strand address two principal service delivery settings: home- and classroom-based. Home-based services consist of professionals' going to the child's home to provide help to the family. Sometimes, the actual locale is different; community settings or a relative's house might be used instead of the family's home. The type of help the family receives depends on the profession (discipline), the needs being addressed, and—probably most saliently—the philosophy of the home visitor. Classroom-based services consist of professionals' going to the child's group-care or classroom program. Settings include family day care homes, child care centers, Head Start programs, preschools, and so on. These practices were written to apply to a broad variety of classroom models, from self-contained to inclusive settings.

Key Features

Four theoretical creeds summarize the practices.

Collective responsibility: teamwork

The first creed is that early intervention involves collective responsibility, meaning that teamwork is needed (Allen, Holm, & Schieflebusch, 1978; Bruder, 1996; Campbell, 1987). The notion is that different perspectives make for better decision making and that no one can do everything. The team consists of the individuals needed to conduct assessment as well as the individuals involved in providing services. An inclusive definition would also embrace resource providers who are not professional service providers (e.g., extended family members, community merchants, other parents). The child's guardian(s) are always central team members.

Transdisciplinary

It is not enough simply to have individuals from different disciplines. The second tenet is that a transdisciplinary model of service delivery is recommended (see McCormick & Goldman, 1979). It is important to avoid fracturing services along disciplinary lines. This acknowledges that early intervention involves development, habilitation, and supporting families. Traditional medical-model or school-based-model practices, in which different team members perform largely independently, is antithetical to recommended practices in EI/ECSE. A critical value embedded in transdisciplinary practices is the exchange of competencies between team members. This not only makes intervention more holistic and complete but enhances team members'

It is not enough simply to have individuals from different disciplines.

abilities. The expertise that individual members bring to a team is vital; without it, the team lacks specificity, resources, and the wisdom of knowledge accumulated through a field of concentrated study (i.e., a discipline).

Functionality

Whereas the first two creeds pertain to service delivery (how services are provided), the third one pertains to the content of early intervention. The philosophy is that intervention should be functional (see Warren & Horn, 1996; Warren & Rogers-Warren, 1985). The challenge around this creed is the definition of functionality. Largely, we have followed the idea that interventions should be those that are necessary for the child's engagement, independence, and social relationships in the context in which he or she lives and those that are immediately useful to the child. Functionality is stressed to avoid practices that serve the apparent need for some professionals to use their favorite interventions, regardless of the usefulness to the child or the impact on the caregivers. An outcome of this philosophy is that the practices tend to favor those that attack a problem head-on, rather than through circuitous, theory-driven interventions.

Practicality and parsimony for regular caregivers

The fourth creed stems directly from the previous one. Interdisciplinary services should be practical for regular caregivers and should be the simplest possible to implement (see Bricker, Pretti-Frontczak, & McComas, 1998; McWilliam, 1992). This is based on the belief that young children learn through ongoing interactions with their natural environment rather than in isolated lessons or sessions. Therefore, it is not the consultant who has the direct impact on the child; it is the child's natural caregivers (parents, teachers, child care providers, etc.). Specialists need to support these caregivers so the child receives an adequate amount and quality of help in areas determined by the team. Specialists must focus in their suggestions on those activities or strategies that are meaningful and practical to caregivers. Because most issues in early intervention can be addressed in more than one way, specialists from different disciplines need to arrive at suggestions that are compatible with caregivers' resources and desires.

Photo by David Naylor

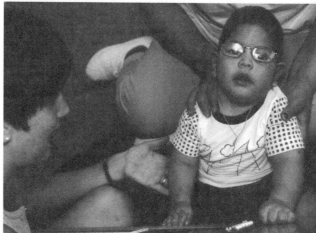

In summary, the practices in this strand emphasize teamwork, loose boundaries between disciplines, functional intervention, and caregivers' accessibility.

Organization of the Practices

The focus group conceived of practices in the major stages of EI/ECSE: first contacts, assessment, intervention planning, and day-to-day services (McWilliam & Winton, 1991). The focus was on the relevance for the most common disciplines involved in early intervention day-to-day services: early childhood special education, early childhood education, occupational therapy, physical therapy, and speech-language pathology (McWilliam, 1996).

Because another strand addressed assessment, most of those practices were transferred to that section. As the Interdisciplinary strand developed, it became clear that some practices were important across contexts. Therefore, it is organized into practices that support working together, cross-disciplinary boundaries, focus on function, and highlight regular caregivers and routines. Supporting this organization is a philosophical bedrock that appears in contemporary discussions of interdisciplinary issues in early intervention. The focus group represented diverse viewpoints. The four themes emerged from the focus group and are supported by the literature.

Definition of Terms

To build the bridge from theory to practice, it is important to define some terms:

Environmental resources and constraints. Interventions are described as being based on environmental resources and constraints, among other factors. This means that they should take into account caregivers' interests and abilities as well as the limitations of the natural physical environments.

Photo by David Naylor

Model of service delivery. In home- and community-based settings, this describes the professional's practices vis-à-vis the child and the parents. It ranges from direct work with the child, through triadic intervention (i.e., the professional, the child, and the parent all working together), to consultation with the parent. In classroom-based settings, model of service delivery describes the professional's practices vis-à-vis the child, the teaching staff, and the other children. A six-model continuum has been defined, from most segregated to most integrated: one-on-one pull-out, small-group pull-out, one-on-one in classroom, group activity, individualized within routines, and pure consultation.

Natural learning environments are the places and activities in which children without disabilities of the same age and their families would participate. This often translates to homes, community settings, child care centers, family day care homes, and preschools.

The **team** consists of the individuals responsible for either assessing or providing services to the child and family, including the parents themselves. (The word parents is used for simplicity to refer to the child's guardians.)

Transdisciplinary service delivery refers to professionals from different disciplines working together, with one of them serving as the primary contact with the family. The primary contact uses strategies that other team members provide, and other team members have direct contact with the family only as necessary (e.g., for assessment, for demonstration). This should not be confused with **interdisciplinary** service delivery, in which numerous professionals work directly with the family and communicate with each other, or **multidisciplinary** service delivery, in which professionals work directly with the family and do not communicate with each other.

chapter 5

Using This Chapter

This chapter should help teams make decisions about how to work together for individual children and families. The practices make it clear that the decisions beginning at the IFSP or IEP meeting and then continuing throughout service delivery are made (a) with families having a meaningful role, (b) with professionals willing to share their expertise (and not reserve it for themselves), (c) in the best interest of child and family functioning, and (d) so that regular caregivers have the support to carry out the family's priorities. Teams can take the practices and create a checklist. An example of such a checklist is found in Chapter 10. Such a checklist can be used for staff development, to guide interagency work, or for various kinds of evaluation.

Another use of the chapter can be to develop a program philosophy around the use of professionals from multiple disciplines. Concerned persons, such as professionals and families, can begin with these practices and form them into philosophy statements by adding "We believe that" at the beginning of each statement. Doubtless, some groups will have issue with some practices, but the very act of defining a philosophy around this topic can be helpful. It can unite a program; it can set expectations for staff, the community, and families; and it can provide guidance for service delivery.

References

Allen, K.E., Holm, V.J., & Schiefelbusch, R.L. (1978). *Early intervention—a team approach.* Baltimore: University Park Press.

Bricker, D., Pretti-Frontczak, K., & McComas, M. (1998). *An activity-based approach to early intervention* (Rev. ed.). Baltimore: Paul H. Brookes.

Bruder, M.B. (1996). Interdisciplinary collaboration in service delivery. In R.A. McWilliam (Ed.), *Rethinking pull-out services in early intervention: A professional resource* (pp. 27-48). Baltimore: Paul H. Brookes.

Campbell, P.H. (1987). The integrated programming team: An approach for coordinating professionals of various disciplines in programs for students with severe and multiple handicaps. *Journal of the Association for Persons with Severe Handicaps, 12,* 107-116.

McCormick, L., & Goldman, R. (1979). The transdisciplinary model: Implications for service delivery and personnel preparation for the severely and profoundly handicapped. *AAESPH Review, 4,* 152-161.

McWilliam, R.A. (1992). *Family-centered intervention planning: A routines-based approach.* Tucson, AZ: Communication Skill Builders.

McWilliam, R.A. (Ed.) (1996). *Rethinking pull-out services in early intervention: A professional resource.* Baltimore: Paul H. Brookes.

McWilliam, P.J., & Winton, P.J. (1991). *Brass tacks.* Unpublished instrument. Frank Porter Graham Child Development Center, University of North Carolina, Chapel Hill, NC.

Stoneman, Z., Cantrell, M.L., & Hoover-Dempsey, K. (1983). The association between play materials and social behavior in a mainstreamed preschool: A naturalistic investigation. *Journal of Applied Developmental Psychology, 4,* 163-174.

Warren, S.F., & Horn, E.M. (1996). Generalization issues in providing integrated services. In R.A. McWilliam (Ed.), *Rethinking pull-out services in early intervention: A professional resource* (pp. 121-146). Baltimore: Paul H. Brookes.

Warren, S.F., & Rogers-Warren, A.K. (Eds.). (1985). *Teaching functional language.* Baltimore: University Park Press.

DEC Recommended Practices: Interdisciplinary Models

Teams including family members make decisions and work together.

. . . .

I1. Families and professionals, including regular caregivers, work as team members in planning, delivering, and evaluating EI/ECSE services.

. . . .

I2. All team members participate in the IEP/IFSP process.

. . . .

I3. Team members are knowledgeable about funding and reimbursement policies and advocate for policies that support recommended practices.

. . . .

I4. Team members support an optimum climate for all caregiving adults to ensure trust, collaboration, and open communication.

. . . .

I5. Team members make time for and use collaborative skills when consulting and communicating with other team members, including families and regular teachers and caregivers.

. . . .

I6. Team members support paraprofessionals so they are treated respectfully and their skills are used most effectively.

Professionals cross disciplinary boundaries.

. . . .

I7. Team members engage in role release (i.e., help others learn each other's skills) and role acceptance (i.e., are prepared to learn others' skills).

. . . .

I8. Team members use a transdisciplinary model to plan and deliver interventions.

Intervention is focused on function, not services.

. . . .

I9. Team members focus on the individual child's functioning (e.g., engagement, independence, social relationships) in the contexts in which he or she lives, not the service.

I10. Team members change models of service delivery (e.g., location) as needed, continuously monitoring what the child can do, what the child is doing, and what the family needs, to decide how to serve them.

I11. Team members select child and family priorities for intervention based on child and family functioning (not services) and determine what is interfering with growth or progress in each priority area.

I12. Team members decide on supports (a) that meet the priorities, (b) that are based on environmental resources and constraints, and (c) that are known to be helpful.

I13. Team members decide on each intervention variable—how to intervene, who should intervene, when the intervention should occur, and where the intervention should occur—based on (a) relevance to the priority (i.e., the functioning the family desires), (b) environmental resources and constraints, and (c) likelihood that it will help.

I14. In IFSPs/IEPs, team members define therapy and specialized instruction to include indirect or consultative services.

I15. Team members use the most normalized and least intrusive intervention strategies available that result in desired function.

I16. Team members use activities within the range of current functioning (i.e., individually appropriate activities).

Regular caregivers and regular routines provide the most appropriate opportunities for children's learning and receiving most other interventions.

I17. Team members plan to provide services and conduct interventions in natural learning environments.

I18. Team members focus on the between-sessions time (i.e., build in activities that can be carried out across time and contexts).

I19. Team members recognize that outcomes are a shared responsibility across people (i.e., those who care for and interact with the child) working with the child and family.

Chapter 6

Recommended Practices in Technology Applications

. . . .

Kathleen Stremel

Technology has the potential to enhance and improve the lives of children and their families. Technology applications also can be important vehicles to improve teaching and learning for children, families, and professionals. The practices presented in this strand include recommendations across three types of technology applications: (a) assistive, (b) instructional/educational, and (c) informational. The 1997 reauthorization of IDEA emphasizes that assistive technology and services be considered for all children identified as having a disability. Assistive technology has been expanded to include what has been traditionally thought of as instructional technology. A child's developmental, educational, and access needs must now be considered by a team to determine the maximum benefits of technology use (Zirkel, 1998). Additionally, the need to operate and maintain medical devices and equipment properly is becoming more of an issue for families and professionals as the number of medically dependent infants increases.

The Technology Applications strand includes general policies, procedures, and recommended practices based on research. The strand emphasizes that decision making should be family centered and guided by principles of individualization. The strand does not focus on specific devices, services, funding, or outcomes.

Key Features

. . . .

It is important that assistive technology be *considered* for every child as the IFSP and IEP are being developed. Technology applications should be considered across the following areas to enhance child development and access to natural learning opportunities

Focus group members: Darbi Breath, Lise Fox, Ann Hains, Mark Innocenti, Joan Karp, John Killoran, and Kathleen Stremel

and the typical curriculum (a) motor, (b) cognitive/perceptual, (c) communication/ language, (d) medical, (e) social interactions, (f) adaptive, (g) daily life skills, (h) play, and (i) academic (Lesar, 1998). Additionally, cultural and family preferences must be incorporated into the assessment, funding, implementation, and evaluation process of decision making around assistive technology services. Considerations for the use of low technology applications should be equal to high technology applications. Both technologies have the potential to assist infants, toddlers, and young children to be successful in natural environments, typical settings, and in the general education curriculum.

Advances in the development of technology devices, services, and supports have the potential for enhancing the quality of life for young children and their families. These advances and legislative mandates present challenges to the professionals who provide services to young children (National School Boards Association, 1997; U.S. Department of Education, 1998).

Organization of the Practices

The practices are organized across technological applications for children, their families, professionals, and service programs under the following headings

- professionals utilize assistive technology in intervention programs for children,
- families and professionals collaborate in planning and implementing the use of assistive technology,
- families and professionals use technology to access information and support, and
- training and technical support programs are available to support technology applications.

The recommended practices in this strand focus on multiple outcomes, which include, but are not limited to (a) enhancing development across all domains, (b) increasing independence and access, (c) enhancing individualized child and family interaction/instruction, (d) supporting professionals and families to ensure successful intervention and educational results, and (e) increasing family and professional access to information and networking.

The majority of practices focus on the use of technology to impact directly the lives of young children and their families, recognizing that the intended outcomes for infants and toddlers will be somewhat different than those for preschool-aged and older children. There is also strong encouragement to use technology at the preservice and inservice levels of personnel preparation to increase competencies of service providers, families, and administrators across the types of technological applications. In the 21st century professionals are using distance technologies to remain current in their areas of expertise, to upgrade their certification, and to collaborate with families and other professionals. As technological application advances continue, there remains a need to validate tools that increase independence and interaction, enhance individual instruction, and lead to meaningful early intervention and early educational outcomes.

Definition of Terms

Assistive technology is defined as any item, piece of equipment, or product, whether acquired commercially, off the shelf, modified, or customized, that is used to increase, maintain, or improve the functional capabilities of individuals with disabilities (PL 101-407, The Technology Related Assistance Act of 1988). The IDEA amendments of 1997 focus on expanding access. Thus, assistive technology has been expanded to include instructional technology.

High technology (high tech) and **low technology** (low or light tech) are general terms that are used by researchers and educators. High technology usually refers to complex electrical and electronic devices, such as computers, voice synthesizers, Braille readers, augmentative communication systems, and environmental control units. Low technology refers to more simple devices; supports; systems; and adaptations such as custom-designed hand tools, positioning devices, and other simple, inexpensive, easy-to-use devices (Galvin & Scherer, 1996).

The terms **distance education**, **distance learning**, and **distributed learning** refer to a system in which educator and learner are separated by physical distance; the concept is that distance education systems may bring together, in virtual space, learners, educators, and curriculum materials that are distributed throughout a wide arena, perhaps the whole globe.

chapter
6

Using This Chapter

The practices in this strand were developed primarily for service programs and professionals. However, families also can benefit significantly from the practices as they are central partners in the development and implementation of the IFSP and IEP. It is critical that the entire educational team considers the maximum benefits of the use of technology for each individual child. Families and professionals must realize that technology is only a tool, not a solution. Review and discussion of these practices can help program personnel better understand their current capabilities as well as their training needs.

It is critical that the entire educational team considers the maximum benefits of the use of technology for each individual child.

References

Galvin, J.C. & Scherer, M.J. (1996). *Evaluating, selecting, and using appropriate assistive technology.* Gaithersburg, MD: Aspen.

Lesar, S. (1998). Use of assistive technology with young children with disabilities: Current status and training needs. *Journal of Early Intervention, 21,* 146-159.

National School Boards Association (1997). *Technology for students with disabilities: A decision-maker's resource guide.* Alexandria, VA: Author.

U.S. Department of Education, Office of Special Education Programs (1998). Integrating technology into the standard curriculum. *Research Connections, 3,* 1-8.

Zirkel, P. (1998). Assistive technology: What are the legal limits? *The Special Educator, 2*(5), 4.

DEC Recommended Practices: Technology Applications

Professionals utilize assistive technology in intervention programs for children.

. . . .

T1. Service agencies and personnel training programs use technology as a vehicle for more effectively serving children, families, and professionals.

. . . .

T2. State agencies arrange for leaders/teams to provide program staff with assistive and instructional technology as well as training and support for technology.

. . . .

T3. Service programs and professionals provide assistive technology for improving early intervention/early childhood special education services for all children with disabilities in order to increase:
- Communication and Language
- Environmental Access
- Social-Adaptive Skills
- Mobility and Orientation Skills
- Daily Life Skills
- Social Interaction Skills
- Health
- Position/Handling

. . . .

T4. Service programs and professionals consider assistive technology applications to increase children's ability to function and participate in diverse and less restrictive environments.

. . . .

T5. Professionals consider chronological age-appropriateness and developmentally appropriate practices for infants, toddlers, and preschool children when selecting types of assistive technology in assessment and intervention.

. . . .

T6. Professionals match assistive technology tools/devices to intervention and instructional objectives and evaluate to determine the effectiveness of the specific assistive technology tool/device.

chapter 6

. . . .

T7. Service programs and professionals consider the least intrusive, least intensive, yet effective low-tech devices in making decisions about assistive technology for individual children.

. . . .

T8. Service programs and professionals consider the use of technology to assist in the assessment process.

. . . .

T9. Service programs and professionals have knowledge of sources for funding and consider procedures to coordinate resources for funding and re-use.

Families and professionals collaborate in planning and implementing the use of assistive technology.

. . . .

T10. Professionals' use and selection of assistive technology is based on families' preferences within assessment, implementation, and evaluation activities.

. . . .

T11. Professionals provide assistance to individual families in the use, maintenance, and generalization of assistive technology to facilitate child development.

. . . .

T12. Professionals and families provide children access to assistive devices across settings. Teachers and parents place the devices/tools in the location where instruction and interaction take place.

. . . .

T13. Service programs and professionals are responsive to the culture, language, and economics of the family when making decisions concerning assessment, funding, implementation, and evaluation for technology applications.

Families and professionals use technology to access information and support.

. . . .

T14. Service programs and professionals provide families choices and opportunities to use technology applications to access information and network with other families for support/advocacy.

. . . .

T15. Professionals and families use technology applications (i.e., teleconferencing and distance learning) to increase their knowledge base and skills.

. . . .

T16. Service programs and family organizations use information technology as a source of resources for families.

. . . .

T17. Professionals have competencies to access technology for obtaining current research, reviewing effective practices, and networking with peers.

Training and technical support programs are available to support technology applications.

. . . .

T18. State agencies and personnel training programs require licensure or credentials, and continuing education units for technology specialists.

. . . .

T19. State agencies, service programs, and personnel training programs infuse technology at the preservice and inservice levels to increase competencies of service providers, families, and administrators in assistive, instructional, and informational technologies.

. . . .

T20. Service programs provide maintenance services for repair and replacement of devices.

. . . .

T21. Preservice/inservice programs provide training across transdisciplinary teams for parent involvement, training and decision making in the area of technology.

. . . .

T22. Service programs provide training and technical support to teachers and parents of specific children for ongoing support, transition, and operational maintenance in the area of assistive technology.

Notes

Indirect Supports

· · · · · ·

Chapter 7

Recommended Practices in Policies, Procedures, and Systems Change

· · · · · · · · · · · ·

Gloria Harbin and Christine Salisbury

Research on the development of organizations and public policy indicates that an adequate *infrastructure* increases the likelihood that recommended practices will be used to deliver services and supports to young children and their families. When quality practices are used consistently it is more likely that children and their families will experience positive outcomes. The interdependent relationships between structure, services, supports, and outcomes are consistent with ecological theories of development (e.g., Bronfenbrenner, 1976; Gallimore, Weisner, Kaufman, & Bernheimer, 1989). These theories suggest that the child's development is influenced not only by the family, neighborhood, subculture, and community, but by the systems of services and supports that serve them as well (Bronfenbrenner, 1976).

The organizational structure, organization, and use of resources, policies, and program procedures within these settings are important elements of the infrastructure that provide the necessary foundation at the local, state, and federal levels for the use of all the DEC Recommended Practices. For this infrastructure to be effective in facilitating the use of recommended practices, there needs to be *coherence and alignment* among the various elements. For example, the infrastructure will be stronger and more effective if the policies require the use of recommended practices, the administrative structure facilitates their use, and the funding and reimbursement mechanisms are also designed to promote recommended practices.

The diverse needs of children with disabilities and their families often cannot be met by a single agency, program, or provider. The need for an integrated system of services and supports creates challenges and adds complexity to the development of an

Focus group members: Gwen Beegle, Barbara Bowman, Michael Conn-Powers, Carl J. Dunst, Jim Gallagher, Corrine Garland, Gloria Harbin, George Jesien, Penny Milburn, Sharon Rosenkoetter, Sarah Rule, Christine Salisbury, and Sharon Walsh

adequate infrastructure *across* agencies and resource supports. The practices contained in this chapter are designed to assist readers in the development of an adequate infrastructure that supports and integrates the recommended practices listed in the other chapters. This chapter also contains suggestions for the processes to be used in developing the infrastructure. The concepts and processes used in this chapter are consistent with those developed by Senge (1990) and others who have recognized the need in organizations for decisions to be made collaboratively and for individuals to view themselves as active participants and life-long learners.

Since most infrastructures at the state and community level do not conform to all of the recommended practices in this book, this chapter also provides suggestions for *system change* practices that can be used to improve the structure and operation of the systems charged with delivering services and supports to children and their families. Constructive system change requires *leadership* that is effective and that operates from a comprehensive plan developed through the collaborative partnerships of those involved with and affected by the changes of the organization.

Organization of the Practices and Definition of Terms

The practices contained in this chapter are divided into six sections. The following provides a description of the key concepts related to the recommended practices in each of the sections.

Families and professionals shape policy at the federal, state, and local levels

Everyone participating in the provision of early intervention/early childhood special education services and supports can and should contribute in some way to developing policies that reflect recommended practices and to improving service systems (Senge, 1990). The recommended practices in this section reflect the need for each person to educate him- or herself about the policy process and to take an active role in that process.

Public policies promote the use of recommended practices

Public policy is defined as the rules and standards that are established in order to allocate scarce public resources to meet a particular social need (Gallagher, Harbin,

Eckland, & Clifford, 1994). Policy includes documents, mechanisms, and processes. Policy documents include not only legislation, but executive orders, rules and regulations, program guidelines, official memos, and interagency agreements. Policy documents exist at the *federal*, *state*, and *local* levels. For example, IDEA is an example of *federal* legislation, and there are federal regulations to further specify the requirements of the legislation. There is also *state* legislation with accompanying regulations; the state special education regulations are an example. At the *local* level, there are local school board policies and individual program policies. Examples of policy mechanisms include use of pilots and demonstration projects, use of requests for proposals (RFPs) to direct actions and resources, interagency planning groups, and training and technical assistance initiatives. Policy evolves through three stages: *policy development* occurs when the documents are being crafted, *policy approval* occurs when the written policies receive official sanction and adoption, and *policy implementation* occurs when the policies are implemented and used.

Program policies and administration promote family decision making, recommended practices, and collaboration

Practices in the three areas of (a) family participation in decision making, (b) promoting the use of recommended practices, and (c) interagency and interdisciplinary collaboration describe how programs should operate to ensure that children and families receive the services and supports they need. Appropriate implementation of these practices will ensure that services are flexible and responsive to the diverse needs of children and families, coordinated within and among organizations, and implemented by qualified personnel. In organizations implementing recommended practices, partnerships, and participatory decision making are evident in the development, delivery, and evaluation of program policies and administration. Program plans developed in these organizations represent an integrated, comprehensive array of services and supports designed to be implemented in inclusive and natural contexts. Mechanisms exist within these organizations to allow for the development of flexible service delivery approaches and the regular self-assessment, program evaluation, and subsequent revision of services and supports based upon evidence of how well these approaches are meeting the needs of children and families.

Appropriate implementation of these practices will ensure that services are flexible and responsive to the diverse needs of children and families . . . .

Program policies, administration, and leadership promote program evaluation and systems change efforts

Practices in this area describe the structure and work of organizations as well as the results of effective leadership within these organizations. A leader is anyone who engages in the work of leadership. Leadership requires the redistribution of power and authority, leads to constructive change, and involves the promotion of inquiry and learning among all individuals in the organization (Hargreaves & Fullan, 1998; Lambert, 1998). The work of effective leaders is grounded in their ability to develop effective partnerships; to align policies, structures, and practices to promote change; and to cultivate a culture within their organizations that not only supports, but encourages, data-informed decision making and change (Salisbury, McGregor, & Brinkley, 2000).

Photo by David Naylor

Systemic change requires that we address the interdependence and development of main components of the system simultaneously and focus on understanding the culture of the system as a basis for changing the system. Systems change efforts can be designed to improve efficiency and effectiveness, or to more deeply alter the fundamental ways in which the overall system and its components are conceived, organized, and delivered. These changes often involve a fundamental revision in values, goals, structures, and roles within organizations (Cuban, 1996; Elmore, 1997; Fullan, 1991). Effective leaders guide the substantive changes within organizations and support the reculturing necessary to sustain those changes and produce positive outcomes for children, families, and staff. Research on large scale systemic change affirms the essential role of leadership in guiding change efforts and the need for a culture of inquiry that is collaborative, informed by data, and appropriately supported (Salisbury, Palombaro, & Hollowood, 1993; Salisbury et al., 2000). Changes often are needed in the procedures, structures, and/or design of services to promote the use of recommended practices; to ensure that services are responsive, that they are used by families, and that they change as the needs of children and families change.

Using This Chapter

The adoption and use of the practices in this chapter will enhance the quality of early intervention/early childhood special education services. It is clear that both process and outcome are essential to the development of responsive early childhood intervention programs of support. Based upon our experience and the research literature supporting the items in this strand, there is clear wisdom in the use of participatory decision-making processes for developing and maintaining quality early childhood intervention programs. The capacity of state and local systems to deliver coordinated, comprehensive services to children and families rests, in large part, on the knowledge of policy makers, administrators, practitioners, and parents about what constitutes effective and recommended practices.

At the state level, adoption and utilization of the practices in this chapter implies a willingness to scrutinize current structures, policies, and practices relative to where leaders in the organization would like to be. Examples of implementation of recommended practices would be the aligning of policies within and across departments, changes in the structure of divisions/departments to reflect integrated functions, and the development of new professional practice standards. At the local and program level adoption and use of the recommended practices would be evident in changes in how teams are created; the location, content, and nature of services and supports; and the way in which planning processes and documents are used to stimulate a culture of inquiry and change. Optimizing the participation and inclusion of individuals from within and outside the organization will help ensure that the outcomes are viewed as meaningful and appropriate to the needs of those involved. A sample administrator's checklist for reflecting on these recommended practices for program and policy development is found in Chapter 10.

References

Bronfenbrenner, U. (1976). Ecology of the family as a context for human development: Research perspectives. *Developmental Psychology, 22,* 723-742.

Cuban, L. (1996). Myths about changing schools and the case of special education. *Remedial and Special Education, 17*(2), 75-82.

Elmore, R.F. (1997). Organizational models of social program implementation. *Public Policy, 26*(2), 185-228.

Fullan, M. (1991). *The new meaning of educational change.* New York: Teachers College Press.

Gallagher, J., Harbin, G., Eckland, J., & Clifford, R. (1994). State diversity and policy implementation: Infants and toddlers. In L.J. Johnson, R.J. Gallagher, M.J. LaMontagne, J.B. Jordan, J.J. Gallagher, P.L. Hutinger, & M.B. Karnes (Eds.), *Meeting early intervention challenges* (pp. 235-250). Baltimore: Paul H. Brookes.

Gallimore, R., Weisner, T.S., Kaufman, S.Z., & Bernheimer, L.P. (1989). The social construction of ecocultural niches: Family accommodation of developmentally delayed children. *American Journal on Mental Retardation, 94*(3) 216-230.

Hargreaves, A., & Fullan, M. (1998). *What's worth fighting for out there?* New York: Teachers College Press.

Lambert, L. (1998). *Building leadership capacity in schools.* Alexandria, VA: ASCD.

Salisbury, C., Palombaro, M.M., & Hollowood, T.M. (1993). On the nature and change of inclusive schools. *Journal of the Association for Persons with Severe Handicaps, 18*(2), 75-84.

Salisbury, C., McGregor, G., & Brinkley, J. (2000). The administrative climate and context of inclusive elementary schools. Working paper. *Principal's Project.* Erikson Institute, Chicago, IL.

Senge, P.M. (1990). *The fifth discipline.* New York: Currency Doubleday.

DEC Recommended Practices: Policies, Procedures, and Systems Change

Families and professionals shape policy at the federal, state, and local levels.

. . . .

PS1. Families and professionals educate themselves about public policies and the policy development process and contexts (laws, regulations, etc.) and the key players at the federal, state, and local levels and advocate for consistent federal, state, and local policies that reflect recommended practices.

. . . .

PS2. Families and professionals participate in advocacy and public policy making in a variety of ways including: public awareness, creating coalitions, participating in task forces that revise or develop policies, and creating a unified community vision for children and families.

. . . .

PS3. Families and professionals use and translate research data to educate themselves, the public, and decision makers about the importance of services provided in accordance with recommended practices.

. . . .

PS4. Families and professionals analyze and explore policy options and the possible consequences of those options.

Public policies promote the use of recommended practices.

. . . .

PS5. State and local policies and procedures are in compliance with federal policies (who, what, when, and where, the "musts" and the "shoulds") as well as recommended practices (e.g., identification for services is based on the educational needs of the child, not on cognitive referencing or the availability of resources).

. . . .

PS6. Public policies require an adequate infrastructure for appropriate services based on recommended practice (administration, funding, salaries, staffing, personnel standards, training and leadership development, research and program evaluation, model or pilot programs, and technical assistance).

PS7. Public policies provide for sufficient, alternative, flexible fiscal and administrative requirements that facilitate: (a) the effective use of natural and inclusive settings, (b) interagency coordination at the "systems" level, and (c) interdisciplinary collaboration at the "direct-service" level (Medicaid waivers, child care subsidies, blended funding, itinerant services, etc.)

PS8. Public policies reflect family support principles across all systems of services, birth through 5 (e.g., providing service coordination for children birth-5 rather than just birth-2, etc.), including strategies that help to ensure participation of traditionally underrepresented families.

PS9. Public policies create a system of appropriate learning opportunities and environments that take advantage of community resources and inclusive or natural learning environments, not just traditional disability or school-based programs.

PS10. Public polices are examined and revised as needed to ensure that they reflect diversity.

PS11. Public policies require periodic review and revision of policies based upon systematic evaluation of data regarding needs and outcomes.

Program policies and administration promote family participation in decision making.

PS12. When creating program policies and procedures, strategies are employed to capture family and community voices and to support the active and meaningful participation of families and community groups, including those that are traditionally underrepresented.

PS13. Program policies create a participatory decision-making process of all stakeholders including individuals with disabilities. Training in teaming is provided as needed.

PS14. Program policies ensure that families understand their rights including conflict resolution, confidentiality, and other matters.

. . . .

PS15. Program policies are examined and revised as needed to ensure that they reflect and respect the diversity of children, families, and personnel.

. . . .

PS16. Program policies are provided in sufficient detail and formats so that all stakeholders understand what the policy means.

. . . .

PS17. Program policies require a family-centered approach in all decisions and phases of service delivery (system entry, assessment procedures, Individualized Family Service Plan (IFSP)/Individualized Education Program (IEP), intervention, transition, etc.) including presenting families with flexible and individualized options for the location, timing and types of services, supports, and resources that are not disruptive of family life.

. . . .

PS18. Program policies provide for the dissemination of information about program initiatives and outcomes to stakeholders.

Program policies promote the use of recommended practices.

. . . .

PS19. Program policies establish accountability systems that provide resources, supports, and clear action steps to ensure compliance with regulations and to ensure that recommended practices are adopted, utilized, maintained, and evaluated; resulting in high quality services.

. . . .

PS20. Program policies reflect recommended practices including personnel standards, child-staff ratios, group size, case loads, safety, assistive technology, and EI/ECSE services and practices. Incentives, training, and technical assistance to promote the use of recommended practices in all settings are provided.

. . . .

PS21. Program policies support the provision of services in inclusive or natural learning environments (places in which typical children participate, such as the home or community settings, public and private preschools, child care, recreation groups, etc.). Strategies are used to overcome challenges to inclusion.

. . . .

PS22. Program policies ensure that the IFSP/IEP is used on a regular and frequent basis to determine the type and amounts of services, the location of services, and the desired outcomes.

PS23. Program policies provide clear job descriptions and provide for personnel competencies and on-going staff development, technical assistance, supervision, and evaluation to inform and improve the skills of practitioners and administrators.

PS24. Program policies ensure that family supports, service coordination, transitions, and other practices occur in response to child and family needs rather than being determined by the age of the child (e.g., b-2, 3-5).

PS25. Program policies ensure that multiple instructional models are available to meet the individual needs of children (e.g., less structure to more structure, child driven to teacher driven, peer mediated to teacher mediated, etc.).

PS26. Administrators provide for a supportive work environment (e.g., hiring and retention policies, compensation and benefits, safety, workspace, etc.).

PS27. Program coordinators/supervisors have training in early childhood education, early intervention, early childhood special education, and supervision.

PS28. Administrators are affiliated with professional early childhood/early childhood special education organizations and encourage staff to maintain their affiliations. Continuing education, such as staff attendance at meetings and conferences, to enhance professional growth is supported.

Program policies and administration promote interagency and interdisciplinary collaboration.

PS29. Program policies include structures and mechanisms such as job descriptions, planning time, training, and resources for teaming resulting in meaningful participation for on-going coordination among professionals, families, and programs related to service delivery including transition.

PS30. Program policies facilitate and provide for comprehensive and coordinated systems of services through interagency collaboration by clearly delineating the components, activities, and responsibilities of all agencies (e.g., joint policies across agencies; collaborative planning on a system, child, and family basis; shared forms and plans, etc.).

> **PS31.** Program policies result in families and professionals from different disciplines working as a team developing and implementing IFSPs/IEPs that integrate their expertise into common goals.

Program policies, administration, and leadership promote program evaluation and systems change efforts.

> **PS32.** Policies, structures, and practices are aligned to promote systems change.

> **PS33.** A shared vision (of all stakeholders), clear values/beliefs, and an understanding of the culture and context to be changed guide efforts to restructure and reform systems. Decisions about what to change result from regular analysis and evaluation of discrepancies among the vision, beliefs, knowledge, and current practices.

> **PS34.** Assessment of the interests, issues, and priorities of constituent groups guides the selection and direction of leadership and systems change strategies.

> **PS35.** Leadership and systems change efforts produce positive outcomes for children, families, and communities that are responsive to their needs. Evaluation data are used to ensure: (a) service utilization, (b) more efficient and effective supports for children, families, and staff, and (c) appropriate systems change leadership and strategies.

> **PS36.** Leadership capacity, risk taking and shared decision making among professionals and families at all levels of the organization are cultivated.

> **PS37.** Leadership and system change efforts include attention to: timely job-embedded professional development, funding, program evaluation, accountability, governance, program accreditation, curriculum, and naturalistic instruction/supports.

> **PS38.** Leadership and systems change efforts rely on strong relationships and collaboration within and across systems: between consumer and system, across systems that deal with children and families, among components within a system, and among professionals from diverse disciplines.

. . . .

PS39. Leadership is committed and willing to change organizational structures (staffing, schedules, teaming) to be responsive to individual needs.

. . . .

PS40. Change is institutionalized through the development of coordinated management and accountability systems.

. . . .

PS41. Resources are provided for program evaluation that occurs along established time points, incorporating appropriate measurable indicators of progress including child and family outcomes and preferences.

. . . .

PS42. Program evaluation is comprehensive, is multidimensional, and incorporates a variety of methods for assessing the progress and outcomes of change. Evaluation efforts take into account differing cultural, contextual, demographic, and experiential perspectives including those of parents and individuals with disabilities.

. . . .

PS43. Program policies delineate all components of service delivery and provide for tracking and evaluation of all components, including child and family outcomes, to ensure that recommended practices are implemented as intended.

Notes

Chapter 8

Recommended Practices in Personnel Preparation

. . . .

Patricia S. Miller and Vicki D. Stayton

A critical element in the provision of quality services for young children with disabilities and their families is the preparation of qualified personnel to deliver those services (Rose & Smith, 1993; Winton & McCollum, 1997; Yates & Hains, 1997). Personnel preparation in EI/ECSE includes practices in both preservice and inservice education. In this chapter, we will present practices that have been recommended by the field for the preparation of early childhood special educators to work with children with special needs birth through 5 years of age and their families.

In this chapter, there is a section of recommended practices for the *delivery* or *process* of preservice and inservice education programs. In the Supplement to this chapter the reader will find standards for *content* of preparation programs (DEC, NAEYC, & ATE, 1995). These two sets of practices (process and content) have been developed and validated separately, but should be considered together when used as a guide for personnel preparation programs.

Early childhood special educators provide services in a variety of roles and settings. The early childhood special educator may work directly with children who have disabilities and their families or may work in a collaborative relationship with other professionals. Settings for service delivery include, but are not limited to, the home, public and private child care, Head Start, public and private school special classes and inclusive classes, hospital settings, specialized agency programs, and other community settings. Specialized areas of preparation for early childhood special educators include the development and implementation of intervention plans and strategies, in-depth competence in developing and conducting assessment procedures, competence in initiating and conducting interdisciplinary planning teams, coordinating interagency services for

---

Focus group members: Vivian Correa, Laurie Dinnebeil, Jeanette McCollum, Patricia S. Miller, Sarah Rule, Vicki D. Stayton, Amy Whitehead, and Barbara Wolfe

families, assessing family resources and needs, and serving as an advocate for children and families (DEC, NAEYC, & ATE, 1995).

Recommended practices in personnel preparation for early childhood education and intervention evolved significantly over the last decade of the 20th century despite the relative scarcity of data-based decisions guiding innovation and change. To a large extent, inservice and preservice preparation practices in EI/ECSE have been influenced more by policy, legislation, and philosophy than by empirical data (Snyder & McWilliam, 1999).

While little research currently exists to guide preservice teacher preparation in early childhood education and early childhood special education (Bredekamp, 1996; Miller & Losardo, in press), research into practices for preservice training and consultation is growing (Wesley, Buysse, & Keyes, 2000).

> *Recommended practices in personnel preparation for early childhood education and intervention evolved significantly over the last decade of the 20th century. . . .*

Key Features

Both preservice and inservice preparation practices reflect several prominent features of an inclusive philosophy toward direct services for children and families and toward preparing providers of those services. Over the last decade, preferred professional preparation practices were characterized by (a) greater participation of families in the planning and delivery of training activities, (b) an increase in the crossing of discipline boundaries to access appropriate preservice and inservice education and training, (c) greater emphasis on preservice and inservice educational opportunities that included both early childhood and early childhood special education students, (d) increasing interest in interdisciplinary collaboration among preservice faculty and inservice providers, and (e) support for family-centered preparation practices (Bredekamp, 1992; Bredekamp & Copple, 1997; Burton, 1992; Burton, Hains, Hanline, McLean, & McCormick, 1992; Buysse & Bailey, 1993; Kilgo & Bruder, 1997; LaMontagne, Danbom, & Buchanan, 1998; Miller, 1992; Smith, Miller, & Bredekamp, 1998).

The professional associations of the Division for Early Childhood of the Council for Exceptional Children (DEC/CEC), the National Association for the Education of Young Children (NAEYC), and the Association of Teacher Educators (ATE) collaborated to produce sets of professional standards for licensure of educators. The standards incorporated the perspectives of both general and early childhood special education. In addition to a common core of knowledge needed by all teachers of young children (NAEYC, 1996) the literature supports the need for specialized areas of skill and knowledge for professionals who work with young children who have disabilities and their families (Bailey, 1989; McCollum & Bailey, 1991; Odom & McEvoy, 1990; Rose & Smith, 1993; Winton & McCollum, 1997). The content in the areas of specialized skill and knowledge needed by those who work with children who have disabilities is described in the *Personnel Standards for Early Education and Early Intervention: Guidelines for Licensure in Early Childhood Special Education* (DEC, NAEYC, & ATE, 1995). See the Supplement to this chapter.

Professional practice standards have established inclusive services as critical to the development of young children with disabilities (Bredekamp, 1992; DEC, 2000; Odom & McLean, 1996; Strain, 1990). Inclusive services for children and families happen best when the preparation of service providers is inclusive of content and practices across essential disciplines (Bredekamp & Copple, 1997; Burton et al., 1992; Miller, 1992).

Trends in the field and support from the literature led to a rapid growth in the development of interdisciplinary, or blended, teacher preparation programs designed to prepare teachers for inclusive education settings (Blanton, Griffin, Winn, & Pugach, 1997; Miller & Stayton, 1998, 1999). Teacher preparation programs that blend both early childhood education (ECE) and early childhood special education (ECSE) professional practice standards are recognized by national accreditation associations (i.e., NCATE) only if they included all DEC/CEC and NAEYC personnel standards (Bologna et al., 1996). Successful interdisciplinary teacher preparation programs prepare professionals who can select those strategies and practices from both ECE and ECSE that match the needs of a specific child and family (Kilgo et al., 1999; LaMontagne et al., 1998).

Organization of the Practices

The practices are organized into seven categories. Six categories provide practices that are relevant for both preservice and inservice activities; the final category is unique to inservice. Categories for the organization of indicators of recommended practice in personnel preparation are (a) family involvement, (b) interdisciplinary aspects, (c) overall program characteristics, (d) cultural and linguistic diversity, (e) field experiences, (f) characteristics and roles of faculty/trainers, and (g) inservice activities. Each category is headed by a statement that captures the essential elements of the practices.

Definition of Terms

It is helpful to understand the definitions of a few key terms when reading the practices. *Preservice* refers to postsecondary programs at the 2-year, 4-year, or graduate level that lead to entry-level preparation in the field of study and result in a degree and/or licensure in that field. *Inservice* means the process of providing ongoing professional development for professionals and paraprofessionals in a specific discipline with the outcome being enhanced professional practice. The term *student* refers to individuals enrolled in preservice programs. *Staff* refers to participants in inservice programs.

Using This Chapter

The newly revised recommended practices that follow this introduction are designed to provide guidance in the development, implementation, and evaluation of personnel preparation programs. These *process* practices and the *content* standards in the Supplement to this chapter have been validated by the field as essential to professional preparation in EI/ECSE.

The reader is encouraged to use the following recommended practices as guidelines for the critical examination of personnel preparation programs. One will see themes of cultural diversity, collaboration and partnerships, family-centered philosophy, and a belief in making research-based decisions in practice. Implementation of the practices will enhance the knowledge and skills of those who work with or on behalf of young children with special needs and their families.

References

Bailey, D.B. (1989). Issues and directions in preparing professionals to work with young handicapped children and their families. In J. Gallagher, P. Trohanis, & R. Clifford (Eds.), *Policy implementation and P.L. 99-457: Planning for young children with special needs* (pp. 97-132). Baltimore: Paul H. Brookes.

Blanton, L.P., Griffin, C.C., Winn, J.A., & Pugach, M.C. (1997). *Collaborative programs to prepare general and special educators.* Denver, CO: Love Publishing.

Bologna, T., Stayton, V.D., Miller, P., Fader, L., Bredekamp, S., & Weintraub, F. (1996, December). *Update on personnel preparation standards and implications for program and state certification.* Division for Early Childhood Annual Conference, Phoenix, AZ.

Bredekamp, S. (1992). The early childhood profession coming together. *Young Children, 47*(6), 36-39.

Bredekamp, S. (1996). Teacher education curriculum: Early childhood education. In J. Sikula, T. Buttery, & E. Guyton (Eds.), *Handbook of research on teacher education,* (2nd ed., pp. 223-348). New York: Simon & Schuster MacMillan.

Bredekamp, S., & Copple, C. (1997). *Developmentally appropriate practice in early childhood programs* (rev. ed.). Washington, DC: National Association for the Education of Young Children.

Burton, C.B. (1992). Defining family centered education: Beliefs of public school child care, and Head Start teachers. *Early Education and Development, 3,* 45-59.

Burton, C.B., Hains, A.H., Hanline, M.F., McLean, M., & McCormick, K. (1992). Early childhood inter-vention and education: The urgency of professional unification. *Topics in Early Childhood Special Education, 2*(4), 53-69.

Buysse, V., & Bailey, D.B. (1993). Behavioral and developmental outcomes in young children with dis-abilities in integrated and segregated settings: A review of comparative studies. *The Journal of Special Education 26,* 434-461.

Division for Early Childhood (DEC). (2000). *Position on inclusion.* Denver, CO: Author.

Division for Early Childhood (DEC), National Association for the Education of Young Children (NAEYC), & Association of Teacher Educators (ATE). (1995). *Personnel standards for early education and early intervention: Guidelines for licensure in early childhood special education.* Denver, CO: Division for Early Childhood.

chapter
8

Kilgo, J., & Bruder, M.B. (1997). Creating new visions in institutions of higher education: Interdisciplinary approaches to personnel preparation in early intervention. In P.J. Winton, J.A. McCollum, & C. Cattlett (Eds.), *Reforming personnel preparation in early intervention: Issues, models, and practical strategies* (pp. 81-101). Baltimore: Paul H. Brookes.

Kilgo, J., Johnson, L., LaMontagne, M.J., Stayton, V., Cook, M., & Cooper, C. (1999). Importance of practices: A national study of general and special early childhood educators. *Journal of Early Intervention, 22*, 294-305.

LaMontagne, M.J., Danbom, K., & Buchanan, M. (1998). Developmentally and individually appropriate practices. In L.J. Johnson, M.J. LaMontagne, P.M. Elgas, & A.M. Bauer (Eds.), *Early childhood education: Blending theory, blending practice* (pp. 83–109). Baltimore: Paul H. Brookes.

McCollum, J., & Bailey, D. (1991). Developing comprehensive personnel systems: Issues and alternatives. *Journal of Early Intervention, 12*, 195-211.

Miller, P.S. (1992). Segregated programs of teacher education in early childhood: Immoral and inefficient practice. *Topics in Early Childhood Special Education, 11*(4), 39-52.

Miller, P.S., & Losardo, A. (in press). Graduates' perceptions of strengths and needs in interdisciplinary teacher preparation for early childhood education: A state study. *Teacher Education and Special Education.*

Miller, P.S., & Stayton, V.D. (1998). Blended interdisciplinary teacher preparation in early education and intervention: A national study. *Topics in Early Childhood Special Education, 18*(1), 49-58.

Miller, P.S., & Stayton, V.D. (1999). Higher education culture—A fit or misfit with reform in teacher education? *Journal of Teacher Education, 50*, 290-302.

National Association for the Education of Young Children (NAEYC). (1996). *Guidelines for preparation of early childhood professionals.* Washington, DC: Author.

Odom, S.L., & McEvoy, M.A. (1990). Mainstreaming at the preschool level: Barriers and tasks for the field. *Topics in Early Childhood Special Education, 10*(2), 48-61.

Odom, S.L., & McLean, M.E. (1996). *Early intervention/early childhood special education: Recommended practices.* Austin, TX: PRO-ED.

Rose, D.F., & Smith, B.J. (1993). Preschool mainstreaming: Attitude barriers and strategies for addressing them. *Young Children, 48*, 59-62.

Smith, B.J., Miller, P. S., & Bredekamp, S. (1998). Sharing responsibility: DEC-, NAEYC-, and Vygotsky-based practices for quality inclusion. *Young Exceptional Children, 2*(1), 11-21.

Snyder, P., & McWilliam, P.J. (1999). Evaluating the efficacy of case method instruction: Findings from preservice training in family-centered care. *Journal of Early Intervention, 22*, 114-125.

Strain, P.S. (1990). LRE for preschool children with handicaps: What we know, what we should be doing. *Journal of Early Intervention, 14*, 291-296.

Wesley, P.W., Buysse, V., & Keyes, L. (2000). Comfort zone revisited: Child characteristics and professional comfort with consultation. *Journal of Early Intervention, 23*, 106-115.

Winton, P.J., & McCollum, J.A. (1997). Ecological perspectives on personnel preparation: Rationale, framework, and guidelines for change. In P.J. Winton, J.A. McCollum, & C. Catlett (Eds.), *Reforming personnel preparation in early intervention* (pp. 81-101). Baltimore: Paul H. Brookes.

Yates, T., & Hains, A.H. (1997). State perspectives on meeting personnel challenges: Closing the gap between vision and reality. In P.J. Winton, J.A. McCollum, & C. Catlett (Eds.), *Reforming personnel preparation in early intervention* (pp. 27-52). Baltimore: Paul H. Brookes.

DEC Recommended Practices: Personnel Preparation

Families are involved in learning activities.

. . . .

    PP1. Family involvement begins early and continues throughout all aspects of the preservice or inservice program (e.g., co-instructing, planning, evaluating, and providing field experiences).

. . . .

    PP2. Family participants in personnel training represent diversity in race, culture, and socioeconomic status.

Learning activities are interdisciplinary and interagency.

. . . .

    PP3. Community agency and school personnel are involved in the preparation program.

. . . .

    PP4. Preparation includes skill development in interagency collaboration.

. . . .

    PP5. Faculty and other personnel trainers within and across disciplines plan and teach together regularly.

. . . .

    PP6. Students/staff participate in sequenced learning activities and field experiences with students and professionals from other disciplines to learn about their own and other discipline roles and to learn about teaming practices.

Learning activities are systematically designed and sequenced.

. . . .

    PP7. Students receive preparation in the content and practice of their field, (i.e., demonstrate skills and knowledge appropriate to the birth through 5 age group and special needs characteristics).

. . . .

    PP8. The program is based on recommended practices of the field including standards from accrediting agencies and professional associations.

PP9. Recommended practices and professional standards are reviewed systematically and updated in the program periodically, reflecting the dynamic nature of the field.

PP10. A written program philosophy is used as a basis for program structure and experiences, and is available to students and faculty.

PP11. All learning activities across and within courses/modules/experiences are sequenced logically from initial knowledge acquisition to guided application and independent application.

PP12. Faculty and other personnel trainers use a variety of recommended and sequenced instructional strategies and methods.

PP13. Students/staff learn to apply instructional strategies in natural environments.

PP14. Faculty and other personnel trainers design learning experiences within courses and field placements that teach students to be reflective and to engage in systematic processes of reflection and self-knowledge acquisition.

Learning activities include study of cultural and linguistic diversity.

PP15. Students/staff participate in activities in which they increase their knowledge of their own culture and heritage, learn that they are a member of different cultures, and recognize intragroup and intergroup differences among members of different cultures.

PP16. Students/staff participate in activities in which they systematically learn about and from various cultural and linguistic groups in ways that are not stereotypic.

PP17. Students/staff participate in activities in which they acknowledge their own biases and recognize their own culture as being one of many that have equal validity.

PP18. Learning experiences consistently engage students in activities in which they learn how culture, ethnicity, language, and socioeconomic status influence early childhood development and practices.

PP19. Students/staff participate in activities in which they learn to develop and implement intervention strategies that are congruous with and respectful of the beliefs, values, and traditions as well as the preferred/dominant language of families from varying cultural and linguistic groups.

PP20. Students/staff participate in activities in which they learn to recognize the potential "power" differential that may exist between them and the families they serve and learn about issues that may be of concern to specific groups (e.g. racism and prejudice).

PP21. Students/staff participate in activities in which they learn to respect the dignity and the right to privacy of the children and families they serve.

PP22. Students/staff participate in activities in which they learn to balance between supporting the unique cultural and linguistic patterns of families and communities and preparing children to meet societal expectations and to find a meaningful place in American society.

Learning activities/evaluations procedures are designed to meet the needs of students/staff.

PP23. Content is integrated in unified learning experiences across related disciplines.

PP24. Students/staff have choices about how to learn and to be evaluated.

PP25. Students/staff access, read, and engage in discussion about current literature and research in the field.

PP26. The program incorporates various levels and types of evaluation, involving faculty, students, and family members in assessing predetermined course and program outcomes.

PP27. Students/staff acquire knowledge and skills needed to effectively consult with other professionals.

PP28. Faculty and other personnel trainers deliver learning activities or other trainings to help teachers supervise paraeducators and volunteers.

Field experiences are systematically designed and supervised.

. . . .

PP29. Field experiences offer opportunities to practice performance competencies of the discipline.

. . . .

PP30. Field experiences are diverse and are matched to student/staff needs, experiences, and interests.

. . . .

PP31. Field experiences occur in a variety of community-based settings in which children with and without disabilities and their families receive EI/ECSE services, including natural environments and inclusive programs.

. . . .

PP32. Field experiences in homes are planned in collaboration with the family.

. . . .

PP33. Field experiences occur in high quality settings that reflect recommended practices in the field.

. . . .

PP34. Field experiences are jointly supervised by faculty and site personnel with experience and licensure in the field.

. . . .

PP35. Field experiences begin early, are sequenced, and provide opportunities for students to provide direct and indirect services to children and to families.

. . . .

PP36. Field experiences include multiple methods of supervision, including onsite modeling, coaching, feedback, and technological methods.

. . . .

PP37. Community providers, cooperating teachers, and program faculty receive support and guidance from each other.

. . . .

PP38. Field experiences include standards for professional and ethical behavior for students in the program.

. . . .

PP39. Field experiences offer experiences with children and families of diverse racial, cultural, linguistic, and socioeconomic backgrounds.

chapter
8

Faculty and other personnel trainers are qualified and well prepared for their role in personnel preparation.

PP40. Faculty and other personnel trainers show commitment to improved services for community schools, agencies, and families.

PP41. Faculty and other personnel trainers have a strong knowledge base, and are credentialed and experienced in working with young children who have disabilities.

PP42. Faculty and other personnel trainers represent diversity in race, culture, gender, language, and other underrepresented groups.

PP43. Faculty and other personnel trainers participate regularly in experiences that build their knowledge and improve their pedagogical practices.

PP44. Faculty and other personnel trainers model recommended practices in the field.

PP45. Faculty and other personnel trainers produce professional products that contribute to the knowledge of the field.

PP46. Faculty and other personnel trainers have knowledge of content and issues in related disciplines.

PP47. Faculty and other personnel trainers translate content in effective ways to meet individual needs of students.

PP48. Faculty and other personnel trainers model collaboration with others and have successful interpersonal skills.

PP49. Faculty and other personnel trainers mentor students and other faculty.

PP50. Faculty and other personnel trainers serve in leadership and advocacy roles in their community and profession.

chapter

8

PP51. Faculty and other personnel trainers translate current research into practice in teaching and supervision.

PP52. Faculty and other personnel trainers who teach methods courses also supervise field experiences and act as mentors in field experiences.

PP53. Faculty and other personnel trainers use appropriate, research-based preservice and inservice instructional strategies.

PP54. Faculty and other personnel trainers promote practitioner-action research.

PP55. Faculty and other personnel trainers participate as learners and co-constructors of knowledge.

Professional development activities are systematically designed and implemented.

PP56. The curriculum is available in a variety of delivery formats to match the needs of participants.

PP57. Practitioners maintain and expand their skills and knowledge through training that is linked to credits for licensure or other formal credentials.

PP58. The program promotes work-site support by colleagues and administrators for implementing new practices.

PP59. Administrators ensure that training is accessible to participants financially and according to location and schedules.

PP60. Personnel trainers provide follow-up within service delivery contexts.

PP61. Training involves teams of participants, (e.g., general early childhood teachers, early childhood special educators, paraeducators, therapists).

chapter
8

PP62. The program emphasizes meaningful practical content and experiences based on expressed needs of participants.

PP63. Teachers and staff from early education programs and community child care centers are provided with knowledge and skills relative to the inclusion of young children with disabilities.

PP64. Administrators support on-going professional development plans.

PP65. Paraeducators participate in training opportunities that allow for continuing development of skills and knowledge (i.e., tiered or leveled training).

PP66. Paraeducators have opportunities for increased job independence based on more training.

Note: These practices relate to the *process* of personnel preparation. They should be used in conjunction with the DEC standards for the *content* of personnel preparation found in the Supplement to this chapter.

Supplement to Chapter 8

 THE DIVISION FOR EARLY CHILDHOOD

Personnel Standards
for Early Education and Early Intervention:
Guidelines for Licensure
in Early Childhood Special Education

Recommendations of

**The Division for Early Childhood, Council for Exceptional Children
The National Association for the Education of Young Children
The Association of Teacher Educators**

Overview

This paper contains recommendations for licensure for individuals working as early childhood special educators in a variety of settings serving children ages birth through eight with special needs and their families. It has been developed as a part of the ongoing process of clarifying roles and standards for individuals employed in early education and early intervention. These recommendations build upon and extend the prior separate efforts of The Association of Teacher Educators (ATE), The Division for Early Childhood (DEC) of the Council for Exceptional Children (CEC), and The National Association for the Education of Young Children (NAEYC) to generate guidelines for licensure in early education and early childhood special education (ATE & NAEYC, 1991a; ATE & NAEYC, 1991b; CEC, 1992; DEC, 1992; McCollum, McLean, McCartan, Odom, & Kaiser, 1989). The recommendations were derived from a commitment to establishing a shared vision among these key professional organizations in early education and early intervention

for the credentialing of all individuals working with young children and their families.

This paper has several important features. First, the fundamental position of ATE, DEC, and NAEYC, that a free-standing credentialing process is required for persons who work with young children separate from the credentialing of general educators or of special educators, is strongly supported.

Elements of existing position statements from these organizations are incorporated and expanded upon, in response to current indicators of effective practice. Second, the paper offers a conceptual base for identifying the knowledge and skills needed by individuals working with young children, including those with special needs. Third, it provides a framework for clarifying the professional roles in early childhood education and early childhood special education. In particular, the relationship between early childhood educators and early childhood special educators is articulated. Finally, specific content areas around which to organize the licensing of individuals

Note: This concept paper is regularly reviewed to ensure current references and alignment with CEC and NAEYC personnel standards. Check the DEC website (www.dec-sped.org) for updates.

. . . .
Permission to copy not required—distribution encouraged.

working as early childhood special educators in a variety of community settings are described.

The purpose of this concept paper is to provide guidance to states as they develop personnel standards for early childhood special educators. It is intended that these recommendations be reviewed in the context of several companion documents being developed by ATE, DEC, and NAEYC. These companion documents address standards for early childhood educators and articulate implications and guidelines for higher education programs preparing individuals to work with all young children and their families, including those with special needs.

These recommendations should support increased uniformity and unification in preparation, licensure, and practice of early childhood educators and early childhood special educators across states. However, the recommendations should be seen as flexible enough to be applied to the individual variations in licensure practices and service delivery contexts of each state. Individual states must make decisions about who enters the profession, the length of preservice training, the level at which training must occur, and the degree to which integration of early childhood education and early childhood special education can occur in preparation and licensure.

Specific standards for individuals in related service professions are not articulated in this paper. However, it is the position of ATE, DEC, and NAEYC that all individuals who work with children in early childhood settings must possess, to a degree congruent with their roles, the knowledge and skills for working with young children with special needs (ATE, DEC, & NAEYC, 1994). The roles and the unique knowledge and skills required of professionals in related disciplines have been widely discussed (McCollum & Thorp, 1988). Further, a compendium of common core competencies, as well as some discipline-specific competencies, can be found elsewhere (Personnel Committee, DEC, 1992). It remains the responsibility of each profession to establish these standards and to relate them to state licensure or credentialing processes.

Background

There is increasing capacity, nationally, to provide comprehensive, coordinated services for young children with special learning and developmental needs and their families. Federal and state policy initiatives have resulted in more programs for young children in general. With increasing attention to the availability of early education and early intervention services has come recognition of the need to identify standards for practice in providing these services (Bredekamp, 1987; Personnel Committee, DEC, 1992). Further, there is increasing consensus, supported by policy, that the context for service delivery for young children with special needs is the same community setting where their typically developing peers are found. Finally, there is increasing recognition that the changing nature of services to young children requires examination of personnel preparation practices (McCollum & Thorp, 1988; Miller, 1992; Stayton & Miller, 1993). Examination of (a) the structure for licensing individuals who will work in early education and early intervention and (b) the relationship between what often has been seen as the separate fields of early childhood education and early childhood special education is needed (Bredekamp, 1993; Burton, Higgins Hains, Hanline, McLean, & McCormick, 1992).

This paper has been developed as a result of a consensus-building process among the ATE, DEC, and NAEYC. It evolved as a result of informal conversations between these professional organizations, in recognition of their overlapping interests in ensuring high quality environments for all young children, including those with special needs. It is an extension of a position statement cooperatively developed by all three organizations, presented for feedback and review to their respective memberships, and approved during 1993-1994 by each organization's executive board (ATE, DEC, & NAEYC, 1994).

These professional organizations have long recognized their roles in recommending standards for credentialing individuals who work with young children. ATE and NAEYC have an approved position on licensure of early childhood teachers (ATE & NAEYC, 1991a). In 1991, these

chapter
8

organizations began the process of developing guidelines for early childhood special educators that would be congruent with this existing position (ATE & NAEYC, 1991b). DEC has an approved position providing recommendations for licensure of early childhood special educators (ATE, DEC, & NAEYC, 1993) and has compiled professional competencies for early intervention personnel (Personnel Committee, DEC, 1992). Furthermore, the Council for Exceptional Children (CEC) has identified common core knowledge and skills for all special education teachers (CEC, 1992) and is currently engaged in the process of identifying knowledge and skills necessary for teachers to practice within particular specialty areas (CEC, 1993). For the specialty area of early childhood special education, DEC's recommendations for licensure will be incorporated in the CEC documents.

Each of these positions has been used in the development of state credentialing standards (Fore, 1992; Thorp & Fader, 1993). However, there is wide variation in state standards, their existence, the ages of children covered, and the roles and settings to which they apply (Bredekamp, 1993; Thorp & Fader, 1993; NECTAS, 1992). Only a few states have adopted licensure standards that demonstrate either a clear relationship between early childhood educators and early childhood special educators or the unification of those fields in a single license (Thorp & Fader, 1993). As standards for practice have been clarified (Bredekamp, 1987; Bredekamp & Rosegrant, 1992; DEC Task Force on Recommended Practices, 1993), and as children with disabilities receive services in inclusive community settings, it has become clear that there is a need to identify standards to ensure that individuals are available and adequately prepared to work with young children in these new contexts. ATE, DEC, and NAEYC, therefore, acknowledged the need to revisit their current positions and develop a joint position on the qualifications required of all personnel who work with young children, including those with special needs. It is expected that this collaborative process will have several desirable outcomes: (a) the coherence of

state credentialing guidelines, including clearer articulation of the roles of early childhood educators and early childhood special educators; (b) congruence between personnel standards and standards of recommended practice in early childhood service delivery; (c) the increased probability that services to young children with disabilities are delivered in the context of services to all young children; and (d) those services are provided by personnel prepared to provide high quality programs appropriate for all young children.

The recommendations contained in this paper support and expand upon the prior positions of ATE, DEC, and NAEYC. The content of the recommended standards is compatible with existing standards. Standards have been elaborated upon, however, to describe outcomes expected of candidates for licensure, to be congruent with categories driving guidelines for NCATE accreditation of teacher education programs, and to incorporate current conceptions of attributes of high quality programs. These recommendations were derived from two sources: (a) an analysis of the roles currently necessary to support early education and early intervention for young children with disabilities in inclusive community settings where typically developing young children are also served and (b) an analysis of the relationship between the role of early childhood educators and early childhood special educators in these settings. In an evolving field, it is essential to modify recommendations for licensure to address those changes. Similarly, the recommendations provided in this paper will require periodic review and revision.

Conceptual Base Guiding Personnel Recommendations

ATE, DEC, and NAEYC recommend that personnel standards be derived from empirically defensible knowledge and clearly articulated philosophical assumptions about what constitutes effective early education and early intervention for young children with special needs and their families. These areas of consensus represent current recommended practice in the fields of early education and early intervention. This knowledge base and set of philosophical assumptions have, in turn, influenced decisions about the recommended structure and content of certification recommendations.

The Uniqueness of Early Childhood as a Developmental Phase

Early education and early intervention evolved from a belief that the characteristics of development and learning of young children are different from those of older children and adults. Thus, programs serving young children should be structured to support those unique developmental and learning characteristics. The personnel in early childhood programs should have a thorough understanding of the developmental needs of young children and of strategies for structuring a supportive learning environment responsive to those needs (Carta, Schwartz, Atwater, & McConnell, 1991; Cataldo, 1984; ATE & NAEYC, 1991a; McCollum et al., 1989). Further, personnel working with young children with disabilities must first recognize that these are young children (Wolery, Strain, & Bailey, 1992) and then bring to the intervention process an understanding of the interrelationship between the development of young children and the impact of disability on development and subsequent implications for intervention (McCollum et al., 1989; ATE & NAEYC, 1991a).

For the purposes of this document, early childhood is defined as extending from birth through age 8. This definition has both a theoretical and a pragmatic rationale. From a theoretical perspective, development is seen as occurring on a continuum, requiring gradual changes in approaches to instruction as development proceeds (McCollum et al., 1989; ATE & NAEYC, 1991a). A program serving infants and toddlers will look markedly different from one serving children aged 5 through 8; yet each will share underlying organizational principles that contrast starkly with programs for older children.

Pragmatically, there are clear benefits to be derived from linking the entire birth through 8 age range, particularly for the two age extremes—birth to 3 and 5 through 8. Current conceptualizations of effective practice with young children were first

proposed as a response to the apparent trend toward downward escalation of curriculum, in particular to the practice of providing formal and academic instruction to young children (Bredekamp, 1987; Bredekamp & Rosegrant, 1992). In order for children in the early primary grades to be taught in a developmentally appropriate fashion, personnel must be prepared to see the link between child development and teaching strategies uniquely structured to respond to that development.

The Significant Role of Families in Early Education and Intervention

Families provide the primary context for young children's learning and development. The central role of families suggests the need for establishing relationships with families that ensure continuity between families and the providers of early education and intervention (Powell, 1994). These relationships should be built upon mutual support of each other's roles, upon a commitment to joint decision-making, and upon respect for families' choices and preferences for their level of involvement (Garshelis & McConnell, 1993; Harry, 1992; McGonigal, Kaufmann, & Johnson, 1991; Vincent, Salisbury, Strain, McCormick, & Tessier, 1990).

The conception of collaboration with families suggests an active role for families, placing them at the center of the educational process, if that is their choice (McLean & Odom, 1993). It represents a logical evolution of the principles of family involvement that have traditionally characterized early childhood services. Current principles differ from traditional principles in intensity and in an increased focus on engaging families in a mutual relationship via family-centered services, rather than as recipients of professional expertise (Bredekamp, 1993; Hills, 1992; McGonigal et al., 1991). Furthermore, it reflects recent changes in public policy (Beckman, Newcomb, Frank, Brown, & Filer, 1991). Part H and, to a lesser extent, Part B of the Individuals with Disabilities Education Act (IDEA, 1990) provide roles for families in assessment, planning, and intervention, as well as in the larger system development process. Family concerns and priorities must be addressed, and intervention must be provided in environments that are meaningful for families (Beckman et al., 1991; McGonigal et al., 1991; Vincent et al., 1990). Professional standards should be developed to ensure effective collaboration with families, derived (a) from an understanding of the experiences of families of young children, including those with disabilities; (b) from a knowledge of specific strategies to establish and maintain productive relationships with families with diverse needs, experiences, and preferences; and (c) from a knowledge of specific legal requirements (Wolery et al., 1992; Beckman et al., 1991).

The Role of Developmentally and Individually Appropriate Practices

Developmentally appropriate practices provide a framework for instructional practices based on the assumption that the opportunities needed for learning and development come primarily from children's active engagement and participation in their environment (Bredekamp, 1987). Thus, developmentally appropriate practices maximize children's opportunities to make choices, value children's interests, and emphasize play and enjoyment. Developmentally appropriate practices encompass practices that are both age-appropriate and individually appropriate. Age-appropriate programs provide for a wide range of interests and abilities within which the chronological age expectation of a typically developing child can be found. Individually appropriate planning is guided by an understanding of the needs and interests of individual children and of the adaptations that may be necessary to enhance learning.

There has been much discussion of the applicability of developmentally appropriate practices to early childhood special education (Bredekamp, 1993; Carta, Atwater, Schwartz, & McConnell, 1993; Carta, Schwartz, Atwater, & McConnell, 1991; Mallory, 1992; McCollum & Bair, 1994; McLean & Odom, 1993). Children with and without special needs have been found to be more actively involved in activities they initiate themselves, in contrast to teacher-initiated activities (Diamond, Hestenes, & O'Connor, 1994). However, achieving a broad enough conception of developmentally appropriate practices that are truly relevant for all young children, including those with special needs, remains a challenge. For

example, when planning for young children with severe disabilities, chronologically age-appropriate practices may differ markedly from developmentally age-appropriate practices. Yet, in many instances the former are necessary for successful inclusion and for the functional development of that child (McLean & Odom, 1993). Furthermore, teacher behavior might best be viewed as occurring on a continuum from highly directive to facilitative instructional behaviors (Bredekamp & Rosegrant, 1992). In judging the degree of support needed by an individual child, it seems critical first to err on the side of less directive strategies and then to consider what is known about the capacity of an individual child to obtain feedback from the environment and from peers when planning for lesser or greater degrees of support (Bredekamp, 1993; Bredekamp & Rosegrant, 1992; Johnson & Johnson, 1992; McCollum & Bair, 1994). Finally, individually appropriate practices for young children with special needs require actively assessing and planning for individual children. Such planning is based upon strengths, needs, and a clear understanding of environmental adaptations that may be necessary for that child to benefit from the environment.

Personnel standards for the early childhood special educator should ensure skillful application of developmentally appropriate practices with all young children and especially those with special needs. Therefore, standards must address the key dimensions of the continuum of teaching strategies; understanding the role of the child, the role of the environment, the behavioral expectations of typically developing peers, and the role of the professional.

The Preference for Service Delivery in Inclusive Settings

Young children with special needs are increasingly receiving services in integrated settings along with their typically developing peers. Both Part B and Part H of IDEA (1990) support early intervention and education in inclusive settings. Specifically, infants and toddlers must receive services in normalized, natural environments, and preschoolers with special needs must receive services in the least restrictive environment. The regulations for Part H

chapter

8

define natural environments as "settings that are natural and normal for the child's age peers who have no disability," including home and community settings. Based on the least restrictive environment principle, states must ensure that

"to the maximum extent appropriate, children with disabilities, including children in public or private institutions and other care facilities, are educated with children who are not disabled, and that special classes, separate schooling, or other removal of children with disabilities from the regular education environment occurs only when the nature or severity of the disability is such that education in regular classes with the use of supplementary aids and services cannot be achieved satisfactorily" [IDEA, 1990, 1412(5)].

DEC and NAEYC (1993) identified inclusion as the preferred service delivery option for young children with special needs. This practice of inclusion is based on the belief that young children with special needs are more similar to their peers than different from them, and that all young children benefit from learning together as members of a diverse community. The strength of the movement to provide services to young children in normalized community settings provides the incentive for developing a unified statement on professional standards.

Because inclusion is the preferred option, all professionals working with young children need to be sufficiently knowledgeable about the needs of young children with disabilities and about appropriate interventions with them in order to provide age appropriate and individually appropriate services to all of the children with whom they work. Professionals must also be prepared to work in the diverse range of community settings in which young children and families receive services. Some professionals now argue that for the full inclusion of infants, toddlers, and preschoolers with special needs to occur, personnel preparation programs should combine early childhood and early childhood special education (Bredekamp, 1992; Burton et al., 1992; Miller,

1992; Odom & McEvoy, 1990). In addition, a commitment to inclusionary practices requires the delineation of a range of roles from early childhood educator to early childhood special educator, as well as a delineation of professional standards for these roles.

The Importance of Culturally Competent Professional Behavior

All development and learning occurs within and is influenced by a cultural context. Because of the great diversity within our communities and among and within families, professionals working with young children should be prepared to provide culturally competent services. Arcia, Keyes, Gallagher, and Herrick (1993) reported that approximately 32% of children under age 5 in the United States are of ethnic minority. In some states, this percentage is approaching or has already reached majority status. Research suggests, however, that the majority of early interventionists are Caucasian (Christensen, 1992). Whereas African Americans are relatively well-represented in the staff of early childhood programs (Kisker, Hofferth, Phillips, & Farquhar, 1991), they remain the minority of total staff. With this discrepancy between the cultural and ethnic status of consumers and providers of services, it is imperative that specific knowledge and skills be articulated to enable individuals working with young children and families to approach diversity in an effective manner within the context of the service delivery setting.

PL 102-119 extended services to typically under-served groups, including cultural and ethnic minority groups, by requiring states to develop policies and practices with families that ensure access to culturally competent services within the community. Roberts (1990) defined cultural competence as "a set of congruent behaviors, attitudes, and policies that come together in a system, agency, or among professionals to enable that system, agency, or those professionals to work effectively in cross-cultural situations" (p. 15). DEC's recommended practices for personnel competence indicate that cultural and ethnic diversity must be addressed in both didactic program content and through field experiences to prepare professionals to respect the diversity of cultures found in a

chapter
8

community, through intervention practices and policies (DEC Task Force on Recommended Practices, 1993). To work effectively with culturally diverse families, professionals must be knowledgeable about their own cultural background; acquire general knowledge of specific cultures, including those cultures' beliefs about disability, child-rearing practices, and professionals; be aware of the verbal and nonverbal communication styles used in various cultural contexts; understand how their own cultural beliefs and values have an impact on their interactions with families (Christensen, 1992; Hanson, Lynch, & Wayman, 1990; Lynch & Hanson, 1992); and be aware of the impact of policies and practices upon children and families from cultural and ethnic minority groups.

The Importance of Collaborative Interpersonal and Interprofessional Actions

With the implementation of family-centered services and the inclusion of young children with special needs in general community settings, personnel need to be able to work collaboratively with family members, with others in their own discipline, and with individuals from other disciplines as members of teams. IDEA 1990 has provided states with regulations supporting collaboration among disciplines and with families. This shift in service delivery has resulted in the need for early childhood special educators to adjust their roles from the primary role of direct service provider to one of more indirect service delivery, such as, consultant, technical assistant, and staff development specialist (Buysse & Wesley, 1993; File & Kontos, 1992).

In service delivery roles that are even more indirect, the early childhood special educator must possess knowledge and skills required for direct service delivery to consult effectively with colleagues who work on an ongoing basis with children and families. In addition, early childhood special educators must develop skills in building interpersonal relationships, communicating with early childhood educators and related services professionals, and providing technical assistance/training to others (Buysse & Wesley,

1993; File & Kontos, 1992). It is also imperative that the early childhood special educator be knowledgeable about the philosophical base, methodological approaches, and terminology of the disciplines with which collaboration/consultation occur (File & Kontos, 1992; McCollum & Thorp, 1988). The need for this type of knowledge provides a rationale for interdisciplinary preservice training programs. The interagency organization of early childhood services within communities also establishes a rationale for interdisciplinary preservice programs that effectively prepare professionals for collaborative roles.

A Framework for Clarifying Professional Roles

Individuals who work with children in early childhood settings must possess, to a degree congruent with their roles, the knowledge and skills for working with young children with special learning and developmental needs and their families. Personnel standards must support the practice of inclusion, the provision of services for young children with special needs in general early childhood programs and other community-based settings in which typically developing young children are also served. Personnel standards should also support the trend toward the development of combined early childhood and early childhood special education teacher training programs and state licensure that incorporates all recommended personnel standards from DEC and NAEYC. These personnel standards are necessary for individuals functioning in a variety of roles, including but not limited to (a) early childhood educators, (b) early childhood special educators, and (c) related services professionals.

Early Childhood Educator

Early childhood educators should possess a common core of knowledge and skills that includes content specific to young children, birth through age 8, both with and without disabilities. This content includes child development and learning, curriculum development and implementation, family and community relationships, assessment and evaluation, and professionalism with appropriate field experiences through which to apply this content. The early childhood educator may work directly with children birth through age 8, including children with a range of abilities and special needs, and work collaboratively with families and other professionals. This work may occur in a variety of settings such as public and private schools and centers, homes, and other facilities in which children within this age range and their families are served. In addition to the traditional role of teacher, the early childhood educator may assume a variety of roles that require specialized knowledge and skills, including but not limited to early childhood subject area teacher, parent education coordinator, social service coordinator, education coordinator, program administrator, and early childhood unit administrator (NAEYC, 1992; 1994).

Early Childhood Special Educator

Early childhood special educators should also possess a common core of knowledge and skills with the early childhood educator as well as specialized knowledge and skills regarding young children birth through age 8 with special needs and their families. This content includes child development and learning, curriculum development and implementation, family and community relationships, assessment and evaluation, and professionalism with appropriate field experiences through which to apply this content. The early childhood special educator may work directly with children with special needs who are in this age range or work in a collaborative relationship with early childhood educators, family members, and other professionals serving young children with special learning and developmental needs and their families. The early childhood special educator may provide services in both public and private schools and in centers, homes, hospitals, and other facilities in which young children and their families are served. Bricker (1989) discussed five major roles for early childhood special educators: conceptualizer, synthesizer, instructor, evaluator, and listener. The conceptualizer has a broad conceptual knowledge base of developmental processes and curricular domains. This broad conceptual base allows for flexibility in adapting for children with special needs. The synthesizer actively seeks input from other professionals and coordinates this

information in planning programs and service delivery strategies for children and families. The instructor role encompasses direct work with children who have special needs, collaboration with families, and training for ancillary program staff. The evaluator develops an evaluation system that assesses outcomes of children and families and provides mechanisms for reporting to staff. The listener role is a support role for the family. It includes communication skills such as listening, questioning, and problem-solving.

In an investigation of roles across 10 disciplines, Bailey (1989) identified roles specific to early interventionists with a special education background. These roles were: (a) to assess children's development; (b) to plan intervention programs; (c) to implement intervention services; (d) to coordinate interdisciplinary services; (e) to follow-through with recommendations from consultants; (f) to assess family resources, priorities, and concerns; (g) to plan and implement services for families; (h) to coordinate interagency services; (i) to conduct program evaluation; and (j) to serve as an advocate for children and families. Although delineated differently, it seems that the roles Bailey specified identify activities that can be subsumed under the broader conceptual role categories described by Bricker (1989) and can serve as a foundation for the content in these professional guidelines. It also seems apparent that these role categories are very similar to those assumed by the early childhood educator. Differences in the early childhood educator and early childhood special educator's roles arise, however, when one examines the manner and degree to which they implement each role. For example, the early childhood educator's primary roles in conducting assessment may be in conducting screening or in using informal procedures such as observation, whereas the early childhood special educator performs those assessment activities and, in addition, conducts diagnostic assessment, employing criterion-referenced measures for instructional programming, and synthesizes results into written reports.

As discussed earlier, with the shift in service delivery toward family-centered services and inclusion, the early childhood special educator is being required to shift roles from that of primarily providing direct services to indirect service delivery.

When direct services are provided by the early childhood special educator, they are likely to be delivered within an inclusion model as a team member (e.g., team teaching) or as a lead teacher, serving children both with and without special needs (i.e., reverse mainstreaming). Indirect service delivery roles continue to require the early childhood special educator to possess knowledge and skills in the roles identified by Bailey (1989) and Bricker (1989) to serve effectively as a consultant, collaborator, parent educator, program administrator, and staff development specialist for family members, other professionals, and paraprofessionals. In states that have adopted unified licensure requirements, the early childhood special educator should be a key team member who will typically assume more indirect service delivery roles such as consulting/collaborating with early childhood educators and related services professionals to ensure appropriate services for young children with special needs and their families.

Related-Services Professionals

Related-services professionals represent a variety of professional disciplines (e.g., physical therapy, occupational therapy, speech/language pathology, nursing, social work); they provide consultation and support to families and other professionals as well as direct services for children birth through age 8 with special needs. Related-services professionals should also possess a common core of knowledge and skills specific to young children with special needs and their families, along with specialized knowledge and skills in their own professional discipline.

Structure of Recommended Early Childhood Special Education Licensure

It is the intention of ATE, DEC, and NAEYC (1994) to provide a framework for personnel standards that is sufficiently flexible to allow states to plan within the context of local limitations, while also maintaining content-congruence (ATE & NAEYC, 1991b) with the philosophy and assumptions discussed previously in this paper. In developing a structure for licensure standards, the following are recommended:

1. State agencies should develop freestanding standards for licensure; that is, they should separate from existing general education elementary or secondary licenses and from existing elementary or secondary special education licenses (ATE, DEC, & NAEYC, 1994). This recommendation is based on the professional recognition that both early childhood and early childhood special education have distinctive knowledge bases that should drive the preparation of personnel for those fields (ATE & NAEYC, 1991b; McCollum et al., 1989). These licensure standards should apply to all individuals who work with young children with special needs and their families, including early childhood educators, early childhood special educators, and related services professionals.

2. These licensure standards should encompass birth through age 8 as the early childhood developmental period. Arguments have been made for entirely separate credentialing and training for those working with infants and toddlers. However, the most current regulations for Part H and Part B of PL 102-119 appear to lend support to avoiding an artificial demarcation between birth through age 3 vs. 3 through age 5 licensure, by adopting a more seamless perspective on services to young children. The legislation includes attention to transition and continued use of the IFSP throughout the preschool years. Linking the personnel requirements of Part H and Part B at the state level should ensure a commonality of philosophy and practices that would enable more seamless transitions between Part H and Part B services. This broad approach to defining early childhood should minimize implementation problems; enhance the possibility of mobility between roles, settings, and children served; and ensure that professionals are prepared to serve the children and families they are employed to serve. At the same time, recognizing that it is difficult to prepare individuals in a preservice program to be competent across the entire birth through 8 age range, licensure standards should support age-related subspecialties within a broader licensure pattern that may include at least two adjacent age spans (i.e., infant/toddler

chapter
8

and preprimary or preprimary and primary school age).

3. Reciprocal licensure agreements across states should be developed to ensure the easy mobility of personnel and to ensure uniform standards. Reciprocal licensure agreements imply both age and content congruence across the United States.

4. Separate licenses for the early childhood educator and early childhood special educator should be clearly linked so as to encourage professional mobility between roles. This suggests the development of a career lattice (Bredekamp & Willer, 1992) within states that supports not only the upward mobility of professionals within a system but also the horizontal movement of professionals from one setting to another (e.g., Head Start to public school to child care), with comparable responsibilities and compensation. The linkage of separate licensures also supports the option for unified early childhood/early childhood special education personnel preparation programs.

Content Standards for Early Childhood Special Education Licensure

Licensure standards for the early childhood special educator must articulate the common core of knowledge and skills required for all persons who work with young children with special needs and their families as well as specialization knowledge and skills. The common core of knowledge and skills should be derived from the fields of early childhood education, early childhood special education, and special education, with the specialization knowledge and skills based on the knowledge base from early childhood special education. The content of licensure standards must be congruent with the philosophy and assumptions identified in this paper and reflect the spirit and letter of federal regulations specific to serving young children with special needs and their families. Further, licensure standards should be performance-based, rather than course-based. They should ensure that personnel possess the knowledge and skills to work collaboratively as members of family-professional teams in planning and implementing services for young children with special needs in

diverse community settings. Specifically, knowledge and skills should be demonstrated in the areas of (a) child development and learning, (b) curriculum development and implementation, (c) family and community relationships, (d) assessment and evaluation, and (e) professionalism. Application of knowledge and skills should be demonstrated through diverse field experiences.

Licensure standards should reflect the importance of ongoing professional development within state standards. Preservice training should focus on entry-level competence in two age spans of the birth through 8 age range. To become more competent in these subspecialties, to achieve competence in the full age range, or to specialize in a content or ability area, further training is necessary. Licensure standards, therefore, should recognize that graduate-level training is a desirable component of a career lattice for all professionals working with young children with special needs and seeking greater degrees of specialization in early childhood development and service delivery.

Guidelines for Preparation of Early Childhood Special Education Professionals

The competent early childhood special educator demonstrates a common core of knowledge and skills for working with young children with special needs and their families as well as specialization knowledge and skills in at least two of the age subspecialties. The following guidelines describe the specific standards required for the common core and the specialization. These guidelines apply to entry-level licensure whether the training is acquired at the undergraduate or graduate level. These guidelines reflect the philosophy and assumptions discussed previously in this paper and are based on recommended practices derived from theory and research. The guidelines also imply that faculty and supervisors in training programs will be qualified in the area(s) for which they are providing training and supervision. To promote consistency with the *NAEYC Guidelines for Preparation of Early Childhood Professionals* (NAEYC, 1994) and to facilitate states using the option to develop combined certifications, the performance standards include the categories of

chapter
8

(a) child development and learning, (b) curriculum development and implementation, (c) family and community relationships, (d) assessment and evaluation, (e) field experiences, and (f) professionalism.

Basic Guidelines for 4- and 5-Year Institutions (Initial Licensure)

1. **Child Development and Learning Programs prepare early childhood special educators to:**

1.1 Apply theories of child development, both typical and atypical, and apply current research with emphasis on cognitive, motor, social-emotional, communication, adaptive, and aesthetic development in learning situations, family, and community contexts.

1.2 Identify pre-, peri-, and postnatal development and factors such as biological and environmental conditions that affect children's development and learning.

1.3 Identify specific disabilities, including the etiology, characteristics, and classification of common disabilities in young children, and describe specific implications for development and learning in the first years of life.

1.4 Apply knowledge of cultural and linguistic diversity and the significance of sociocultural and political contexts for development and learning, and recognize that children are best understood in the contexts of family, culture, and society.

1.5 Demonstrate understanding of (a) developmental consequences of stress and trauma, (b) protective factors and resilience, (c) the development of mental health, and (d) the importance of supportive relationships.

2. **Curriculum Development and Implementation Programs prepare early childhood special educators to:**

2.1 Plan and implement developmentally and individually appropriate curricula and instructional practices based on knowledge of individual children, the family, the community, and curricula goals and content.

2.1.1 Make specific adaptations for the special needs of children who have unique talents, learning and developmental needs, or specific disabilities.

2.1.2 Develop an IFSP or IEP, incorporating both child and family outcomes, in partnership with family members and other professionals.

2.1.3 Incorporate information and strategies from multiple disciplines in the design of intervention strategies.

2.1.4 Design plans that incorporate the use of technology, including adaptive and assistive technology.

2.1.5 Develop and select learning experiences and strategies that affirm and respect family, cultural, and societal diversity, including language differences.

2.1.6 Plan for and link current developmental and learning experiences and teaching strategies with those of the next educational setting.

2.1.7 Select intervention curricula and methods for children with specific disabilities including motor, sensory, health, communication, social-emotional, and cognitive disabilities.

2.1.8 Support and facilitate family and child interactions as primary contexts for learning and development.

2.1.9 Implement developmentally and functionally appropriate individual and group activities using a variety of formats, including play, environmental routines, parent-mediated activities, small group projects, cooperative learning, inquiry experiences, and systematic instruction.

2.1.10 Develop and implement an integrated curriculum that focuses on children's needs and interests and takes into account culturally valued content and children's home experiences.

2.1.11 Select, develop, and evaluate developmentally and functionally appropriate materials, equipment, and environments.

2.1.12 Demonstrate appropriate use of technology, including adaptive and assistive technology.

2.1.13 Employ pedagogically sound and legally defensible instructional practices.

chapter 8

. . . .

Permission to copy not required—distribution encouraged.

2.2 Use individual and group guidance and problem-solving techniques to develop positive and supportive relationships with children, to encourage and teach positive social skills and interaction among children, to promote positive strategies of conflict resolution, and to develop personal self-control, self-motivation, and self-esteem.

2.2.1 Select and implement methods of behavior support and management appropriate for young children with special needs, including a range of strategies from less directive, less structured methods (e.g., verbal support and modeling) to more directive, more structured methods (e.g., applied behavior analysis).

2.3 Establish and maintain physically and psychologically safe and healthy learning environments that promote development and learning.

2.3.1 Provide a stimulus-rich indoor and outdoor environment that employs materials, media, and technology, including adaptive and assistive technology.

2.3.2 Organize space, time, peers, materials, and adults to maximize child progress in group and home settings.

2.3.3 Implement basic health, nutrition, and safety management practices for young children, including specific procedures for infants and toddlers and procedures regarding childhood illness and communicable diseases.

2.3.4 Implement nutrition and feeding strategies for children with special needs.

2.3.5 Use appropriate health appraisal procedures and recommend referral and ongoing follow-up to appropriate community health and social services.

2.3.6 Identify aspects of medical care for premature, low birth weight, and other medically fragile babies, including methods employed in the care of young children dependent on technology and implications of medical conditions on child development and family resources, concerns, and priorities.

2.3.7 Recognize signs of emotional distress, child abuse, and neglect in young children and follow procedures for reporting known or suspected abuse or neglect to appropriate authorities.

3. **Family and Community Relationships** Programs prepare early childhood special educators to:

3.1 Establish and maintain positive, collaborative relationships with families.

3.1.1 Apply family systems theory and knowledge of the dynamics, roles, and relationships within families and communities.

3.1.2 Demonstrate sensitivity to differences in family structures and social and cultural backgrounds.

3.1.3 Assist families in identifying their resources, priorities, and concerns in relation to their child's development.

3.1.4 Respect parents' choices and goals for children and communicate effectively with parents about curriculum and children's progress.

3.1.5 Involve families in assessing and planning for individual children, including children with special needs.

3.1.6 Implement a range of family-oriented services based on the family's identified resources, priorities, and concerns.

3.1.7 Implement family services consistent with due process safeguards.

3.1.8 Evaluate services with families.

3.2 Collaborate/consult with other professionals and with agencies in the larger community to support children's development, learning, and well-being.

3.2.1 Apply models of team process in diverse service delivery settings.

3.2.2 Employ various team membership roles.

3.2.3 Identify functions of teams as determined by mandates and service delivery needs of children and families.

3.2.4 Identify structures supporting interagency collaboration, including interagency agreements, referral, and consultation.

3.2.5 Participate as a team member to identify dynamics of team roles, interaction, communication, team-building, problem-solving, and conflict resolution.

3.2.6 Employ two-way communication skills.

3.2.7 Evaluate and design processes and strategies that support transitions among hospital, home, infant/toddler, preprimary, and primary programs.

3.3 Administer, supervise, and consult with/instruct other adults.

3.3.1 Employ adult learning principles in supervising and training other adults.

3.3.2 Facilitate the identification of staff development needs and strategies for professional growth.

3.3.3 Apply various models of consultation in diverse settings.

3.3.4 Provide consultation and training in content areas specific to services for children and families and organization/development of programs.

3.3.5 Provide feedback and evaluate performance in collaboration with other adults.

4. **Assessment and Evaluation Programs prepare early childhood special educators to:**

4.1 Assess children's cognitive, social-emotional, communication, motor, adaptive, and aesthetic development.

4.1.1 Select and use a variety of informal and formal assessment instruments and procedures, including observational methods, to make decisions about children's learning and development.

4.1.2 Select and administer assessment instruments and procedures based on the purpose of the assessment being conducted and in compliance with established criteria and standards.

4.1.3 Develop and use authentic, performance-based assessments of children's learning to assist in planning, to communicate with children and parents, and to engage children in self-assessment.

4.1.4 Involve families as active participants in the assessment process.

4.1.5 Participate and collaborate as a team member with other professionals in conducting family-centered assessments.

4.1.6 Communicate assessment results and integrate assessment results from others as an active team participant in the development and implementation of the individual education program (IEP) and individual family service plan (IFSP).

4.1.7 Monitor, summarize, and evaluate the acquisition of child and family outcomes as outlined on the IFSP or IEP.

4.1.8 Select, adapt, and administer assessment instruments and procedures for specific sensory and motor disabilities.

4.1.9 Communicate options for programs and services at the next level and assist the family in planning for transition.

4.1.10 Implement culturally unbiased assessment instruments and procedures.

4.2 Develop and use formative and summative program evaluation to ensure comprehensive quality of the total environment for children, families, and the community.

5. **Professionalism Programs prepare early childhood special education professionals to:**

5.1 Articulate the historical, philosophical, and legal basis of services for young children both with and without special needs.

5.2 Identify ethical and policy issues related to educational, social, and medical services for young children and their families.

5.3 Identify current trends and issues in Early Childhood Education, Early Childhood Special Education, and Special Education.

5.4 Identify legislation that affects children, families, and programs for children.

5.5 Adhere to the profession's code of ethical conduct.

5.6 Serve as advocates on behalf of young children and their families, improved quality of programs and services for young children, and enhanced professional status and working conditions for early childhood special educators.

chapter

8

5.7 Reflect upon his/her own professional practice and develop, implement, and evaluate a professional development plan.

5.8 Participate actively in professional organizations.

5.9 Read and critically apply research and recommended practices.

6. Field Experiences Programs prepare early childhood special educators by having them:

6.1 Observe and participate under the supervision of qualified professionals in a variety of settings in which young children with special needs, from birth through age 8, and their families are served (e.g., homes, public and private centers, schools, community agencies).

6.2 Work effectively with children of diverse ages (i.e., infants, toddlers, preschoolers, primary school-age), with children with diverse abilities, and with children reflecting culturally and linguistically diverse family systems.

6.3 Participate under supervision as an interagency and intra-agency team member.

6.4 Provide consultation services under supervision.

6.5 Demonstrate ability to work effectively during supervised student teaching and/or intensive, ongoing practica experiences (totaling at least 300 clock hours) in at least two different settings, serving children of two different age groups (i.e., infant/toddler, preprimary, or primary) and with varying abilities.

6.6 Analyze and evaluate field experiences, including supervised experience in working with families and with other professionals.

References

Arcia, E., Keyes, L., Gallagher, J.J., & Herrick, H. (1993). National portrait of sociodemographic factors associated with underutilization of services: Relevance to early intervention. *Journal of Early Intervention, 17*(3), 283-297.

Association of Teacher Educators (ATE), Division for Early Childhood (DEC), & National Association for the Education of Young Children (NAEYC). (1993). *Position Statement: Personnel Standards for early education and early intervention.* Reston, VA: Division for Early Childhood/Council for Exceptional Children.

Association of Teacher Educators (ATE) & National Association for the Education of Young Children (NAEYC). (1991a). Early childhood teacher certification. *Young Children, 47*(1), 16-21.

Association of Teacher Educators & National Association for the Education of Young Children. (1991b). Early childhood special education teacher certification guidelines. Unpublished position statement (second draft), November.

Atwater, J.B., Carta, J.J., Schwartz, I.S., & McConnell, S.R. (1994). Blending developmentally appropriate practice and early childhood special education. In B.L. Mallory & R.S. New (Eds.), *Diversity and developmentally appropriate practices* (pp. 185-201). New York: Teachers College Press.

Bailey, D.B. (1989). Issues and directions in preparing professionals to work with young handicapped children and their families. In J.J. Gallagher, P.L. Trohanis, & R.M. Clifford (Eds.), *Policy implementation and PL 99-457: Planning for young children with special needs* (pp. 97-132). Baltimore: Paul H. Brookes.

Beckman, P.J., Newcomb, S., Frank, N., Brown, L., & Filer, J. (1991). *Providing support to families of infants with disabilities.* Manuscript submitted for publication.

Bowman, B. (1992). Reaching potentials of minority children through developmentally and culturally appropriate programs. In S. Bredekamp & T. Rosegrant (Eds.), *Reaching potentials: Appropriate curriculum and assessments for young children* (pp. 128-136). Washington, DC: National Association for the Education of Young Children.

Bredekamp, S. (1987). *Developmentally appropriate practice in early childhood programs serving children from birth through age 8.* Washington, DC: National Association for the Education of Young Children.

Bredekamp, S. (1992). The early childhood profession coming together. *Young Children, 47*(6), 36-39.

chapter
8

Bredekamp, S. (1993). The relationship between early childhood education and early childhood special education: Healthy marriage or family feud. *Topics in Early Childhood Special Education, 13*(3), 258-273.

Bredekamp, S. & Rosegrant, T. (Eds.). (1992). *Reaching potentials: Appropriate curriculum and assessment for young children.* Washington, DC: National Association for the Education of Young Children.

Bredekamp, S. & Willer, B. (1992). Of ladders and lattices, cores and cones: Conceptualizing an early childhood professional development system. *Young Children, 47*(3), 47-50.

Bricker, D.B. (1989). *Early intervention for at-risk and handicapped infants, toddlers, and preschool children.* Palo Alto, CA: VORT Corp.

Bruder, M.B., Anderson, R., Schultz, G., & Caldera, M. (1991). Project profile: Minos Especales Program: A culturally sensitive early intervention model. *Journal of Early Intervention, 15*(3), 268-277.

Burton, C., Higgins Hains, A., Hanline, M.F., McLean, M., & McCormick, K. (1992). Early childhood intervention and education: The urgency for professional unification. *Topics in Early Childhood Special Education, 11*(4), 53-69.

Buysse, V., & Wesley, P.W. (1993). The identity crisis in early childhood special education: A call for professional role clarification. *Topics in Early Childhood Special Education, 13*(4), 418-429.

Carta, J.J., Atwater, J.B., Schwartz, I.S., & McConnell, S.R. (1993). Developmentally appropriate practices and early childhood special education: A reaction to Johnson and McChesney Johnson. *Topics in Early Childhood Special Education, 13*(3), 243-254.

Carta, J.J., Schwartz, I.S., Atwater, J.B., & McConnell, S.R. (1991). Developmentally appropriate practice: Appraising its usefulness for young children with disabilities. *Topics in Early Childhood Special Education, 11*(1), 1-20.

Cataldo, C.Z. (1984). Infant-toddler education: Blending the best approaches. *Young Children,* January, 25-32.

Cavallaro, C.C., Haney, M., & Cabello, B. (1993). Developmentally appropriate strategies for promoting full participation in early childhood settings. *Topics in Early Childhood Special Education, 13*(3), 293-307.

Christensen, C.M. (1992). Multicultural competencies in early intervention: Training professionals for a pluralistic society. *Infants and Young Children, 4*(3), 49-63.

Council for Exceptional Children (CEC). (1992). *Common core of knowledge and skills essential for all beginning special education teachers.* Reston, VA: Council for Exceptional Children.

Council for Exceptional Children (CEC). (1993). Unpublished communication to Division Presidents from CEC Subcommittee on Knowledge and Skills, January 12.

Demchak, M., & Drinkwater, S. (1992). Preschoolers with severe disabilities: The case against segregation. *Topics in Early Childhood Special Education, 11*(4), 70-83.

Derman-Sparks, L. (1989). *Anti-bias curriculum: Tools for empowering young children.* Washington, DC: National Association for the Education of Young Children.

Derman-Sparks, L. (1992). Reaching potentials through anti-bias, multicultural curriculum. In S. Bredekamp and T. Rosegrant (Eds.), *Reaching potentials: Appropriate curriculum and assessment for young children* (pp. 114-127). Washington, DC: National Association for the Education of Young Children.

Derman-Sparks, L. (1993). Revisiting multicultural education: What children need to live in a diverse society. *Dimensions of Early Childhood, 21*(2), 6-9.

Diamond, K.E., Hestenes, L.L., & O'Connor, C.D. (1994). Integrating young children with disabilities in preschool: Problems and promise. *Young Children, 4*(2), 68-75.

Division for Early Childhood (DEC). (1992). Statement to the ATE/NAEYC Commission on Early Childhood Teacher Education, draft submitted by Mallory, February 16.

Division for Early Childhood (DEC) & National Association for the Education of Young Children (NAEYC). (1993). *Position on inclusion.* Reston, VA: Division for Early Childhood/Council for Exceptional Children.

Division for Early Childhood Task Force on Recommended Practices. (1993). *DEC recommended practices: Indicators of quality in programs for infants and young children with special needs and their families.* Reston, VA: Council for Exceptional Children.

Early Intervention Programs for Infants and Toddlers with Handicaps, *Federal Register*, May 1, 1992.

Fenichel, E.S., & Eggbeer, L. (1990). *Preparing practitioners to work with infants, toddlers and their families: Issues and recommendations for educators and trainers.* Arlington, VA: National Center for Clinical Infant Programs.

File, N., & Kontos, S. (1992). Indirect service delivery through consultation: Review and implications for early intervention. *Journal of Early Intervention, 16*(3), 221-233.

Fore, L. (1992). *The relationship between professional recommendations, certification standards and preservice program requirements in Early Childhood Special Education.* Unpublished doctoral dissertation, College of William and Mary, Williamsburg, VA.

Friend, M., & Cook, L. (1992). *Interactions: Collaboration skills for school professionals.* New York: Logmans.

Garshelis, J.A., & McConnell, S.R. (1993). Comparison of family needs assessed by mothers, individual professionals, and interdisciplinary teams. *Journal of Early Intervention, 17*(1), 36-49.

Genishi, C., Dyson, A.H., & Fassler, R. (1994). Language and diversity in early childhood: Whose voices are appropriate? In B.L. Mallory & R.S. New (Eds.), *Diversity and developmentally appropriate practices* (pp. 250-268). New York: Teachers College Press.

Golin, A.K., & Ducanis, A.J. (1981). *The interdisciplinary team: A handbook for the education of exceptional children.* Rockville, MD: Aspen.

Hanson, M., Lynch, E., & Wayman, K. (1990). Honoring cultural diversity of families when gathering data. *Topics in Early Childhood Special Education, 10*(2), 112-131.

Harry, B. (1992). *Cultural diversity, families and the special education system: Communication and empowerment.* New York: Teachers College Press.

Hills, T. (1992). Reaching potentials through appropriate assessment. In S. Bredekamp & T. Rosegrant (Eds.), *Reaching potentials: Appropriate curriculum and assessment for young children* (pp. 43-63). Washington, DC: National Association for the Education of Young Children.

Individuals with Disabilities Education Act of 1990 (IDEA), PL 101-476, 20 United States Code, Secs. 1400-1485.

Johnson, J.E., & Johnson, K.M. (1992). Clarifying the developmental perspective in response to Carta, Schwartz, Atwater, and McConnell. *Topics in Early Childhood Special Education, 12*(4), 439-457.

Johnson, K.M., & Johnson, J.E. (1993). Rejoinder to Carta, Atwater, Schwartz, and McConnell. *Topics in Early Childhood Special Education, 13*(3), 255-257.

Jones, E., & Derman-Sparks, L. (1992). Meeting the challenge of diversity. *Young Children, 47*(2), 12-18.

Kagan, S.L., & Rivera, A.M. (1991). Collaboration in early care and education: What can and should we expect? *Young Children, 47*(1), 51-56.

Kisker, E.E., Hofferth, S.L., Phillips, D.A., & Farquhar, E. (1991). *A profile of child care settings: Early education and care in 1990.* Washington, DC: U.S. Government Printing Office.

Leister, C. (1993). Working with parents of different cultures. *Dimensions of Early Childhood, 21*(2), 6-9.

Lowenthal, B. (1992). Collaborative training in the education of early childhood educators. *Teaching Exceptional Children, 24*(4), 25-29.

Lynch, E.W., & Hanson, M.J. (1992). *Developing cross-cultural competence: A guide for working with young children and their families.* Baltimore: Paul H. Brookes.

Lubeck, S. (1994). The politics of developmentally appropriate practice: Exploring issues of culture, class, and curriculum. In B.L. Mallory & R.S. New (Eds.), *Diversity and developmentally appropriate practices* (pp. 17-43). New York: Teachers College Press.

Mahoney, G., Robinson, C., & Powell, A. (1992). Focusing on parent-child interaction: The bridge to developmentally appropriate practices. *Topics in Early Childhood Special Education, 12*(1), 105-120.

Mallory, B.L. (1992). Is it always appropriate to be developmental? *Topics in Early Childhood Special Education, 11*(4), 1-12.

Mallory, B.L. (1994). Inclusive policy, practice, and theory for young children with developmental differences. In B.L. Mallory & R.S. New (Ed.), *Diversity and developmentally appropriate practices* (pp. 44-61). New York: Teachers College Press.

McCollum, J.A., & Bair, H. (1994). Research in parent-child interaction: Guidance to developmentally appropriate practice for young children with disabilities. In B.L. Mallory & R.S. New (Eds.), *Diversity and developmentally appropriate practices* (pp. 84-106). New York: Teachers College Press.

McCollum, J., McLean, M., McCartan, K., Odom, S., & Kaiser, C. (1989). Recommendations for certification of early childhood special educators. *Journal of Early Intervention, 13*(3), 195-211.

McCollum, J., & Thorp, E. (1988). Training of infant specialists: A look to the future. *Infants and Young Children, 1*(2), 55-65.

chapter
8

. . . .
Permission to copy not required—distribution encouraged.

McGonigal, M.J., Kaufmann, R.K., & Johnson, B.H. (Eds.). (1991). *Guidelines and recommended practices for the individualized family service plan* (2nd ed.). Bethesda, MD: Association for the Care of Children's Health.

McLean, M.E., & Odom, S.L. (1993). Practices for young children with and without disabilities: A comparison of DEC and NAEYC identified practices. *Topics in Early Childhood Special Education, 13*(3), 274-292.

Miller, P.S. (1992). Segregated programs of teacher education in early childhood: Immoral and inefficient practice. *Topics in Early Childhood Special Education, 11*(4), 39-52.

Morgan, J.L., Guetzloe, E.C., & Swan, W. (1991). Leadership for local interagency coordinating councils. *Journal of Early Intervention, 15*(3), 255-267.

National Association for the Education of Young Children (NAEYC). (1992). NAEYC model of early childhood professional development. In *National Institute for Early Childhood Professional Development: Background materials for working sessions.* Washington, DC: Author.

National Association for the Education of Young Children (NAEYC). (1994). *NAEYC guidelines for preparation of early childhood professionals.* Washington, DC: Author.

National Early Childhood Technical Assistance System (NECTAS). (1992). *Section 619 profile, May 1992.* Chapel Hill, NC: Author.

Odom, S.L., & McEvoy, M.A. (1990). Mainstreaming at the preschool level: Barriers and tasks for the field. *Topics in Early Childhood Special Education, 10*(2), 48-61.

Personnel Committee, Division for Early Childhood. (1992). *Compilation of professional competencies for early intervention personnel.* Pittsburgh, PA: Division for Early Childhood.

Powell, D.R. (1994). Parents, pluralism, and the NAEYC statement on developmentally appropriate practice. In B.L. Mallory & R.S. New (Eds.), *Diversity and developmentally appropriate practices* (pp. 166-182). New York: Teachers College Press.

Roberts, Richard N. (1990). *Developing culturally competent programs for families of children with special needs.* Washington, DC: Georgetown University Child Development Center.

Ross, H.W. (1992). Integrating infants with disabilities? Can "ordinary" caregivers do it? *Young Children, 47*(3), 65-71.

Salisbury, C.L. (1991). Mainstreaming during the early childhood years. *Exceptional Children, 58,* 146-155.

Stayton, V.D., & Miller, P.S. (1993). Combining general and special early childhood education standards in personnel preparation programs: Experiences from two states. *Topics in Early Childhood Special Education, 13*(3), 372-387.

Swan, W.W., & Morgan, J.L. (1993). *Collaborating for comprehensive services for young children and their families: The local interagency coordinating council.* Baltimore: Paul H. Brookes.

Templeman, T.P., Fredericks, H.D., & Udell, T. (1989). Integration of children with moderate and severe handicaps into a day care center. *Journal of Early Intervention, 13*(4), 315-328.

Thorp, E.K. & McCollum, J.A. (1988). Defining the infancy specialization in early childhood special education. In J.B. Jordan, J.J. Gallagher, P.L. Hutinger, & M.B. Karnes (Eds.), *Early childhood special education: Birth to three* (pp. 147-162). Reston, VA: Council for Exceptional Children.

Thorp, E.K., & Fader, L. (1993). *Summary of state certification standards for early childhood and early childhood special education.* Unpublished manuscript.

Vincent, L.J., Salisbury, C.L., Strain, P., McCormick, C., & Tessier, A. (1990). A behavioral-ecological approach to early intervention: Focus on cultural diversity. In S.J. Meisels & J.P. Shonkoff (Eds.), *Handbook of early childhood intervention* (pp. 173-195). Cambridge, MA: Cambridge University Press.

Wakefield, A.P. (1993). Developmentally appropriate practice: "Figuring things out". *The Educational Forum, 57,* 134-143.

Wolery, M., Strain, P.S., & Bailey, D.B. (1992). Reaching potentials of children with special needs. In S. Bredekamp & T. Rosegrant (Eds.), *Reaching potentials: Appropriate curriculum and assessment for young children* (pp. 92-111). Washington, DC: National Association for the Education of Young Children.

Acknowledgments

The Division for Early Childhood (DEC) would like to acknowledge the members of the Subcommittee of the DEC Personnel Committee who were involved in the process of developing this concept paper. These individuals reviewed, evaluated, and commented on the initial outline for the paper and each subsequent draft.

Doris Bergen
Department of Educational Psychology
Miami University
Oxford, OH 45056

Carolyn Cooper
Department of Special Education
Eastern Illinois University
Charleston, IL 61920

Elizabeth Erwin
School of Education/ECP
Queens College/CUNY
Flushing, NY 11367-1597

Lora Fader
Department of Special Education
University of Maryland
College Park, MD 20742-1121

John Johnson
Department of Instruction
    & Curriculum Leadership
University of Memphis
Memphis, TN 38152

Jeanette McCollum
Department of Special Education
College of Education
University of Illinois
Champaign, IL 61820

Patricia Major
Department of Special Education
Southern Connecticut State University
New Haven, CT 06515

Bruce Mallory
Department of Education
College of Liberal Arts
Durham, NH 03824-3595

Pat Miller
Education Department
Salem College
Winston-Salem, NC 27108

Pat Nycaard
University of Minnesota
Minneapolis, MN 55455

Georgia Sheriff
Indiana University
Bloomington, IN 47405

Vicki Stayton
Department of Teacher Education
Office of Interdisciplinary
    Early Childhood Education
Western Kentucky University
Bowling Green, KY 42101

Eva Thorp
Early Childhood Special Education
George Mason University
Fairfax, VA 22030

Approved by DEC Executive Board: October 9, 1994
Approved by NAEYC Executive Board: November 29, 1994
Approved by ATE Executive Board: February 21, 1995
Re-affirmed by DEC Executive Board: November 22, 1997
Re-affirmed by the NAEYC Executive Board: April, 1998

Chapter 9

Methods and Activities Used to Produce the DEC Recommended Practices

• • • • • • • • • • • •

Barbara J. Smith, Mary E. McLean, Susan Sandall, Patricia Snyder, and Alison Broudy

As described previously in this book, DEC decided to update and revise the 1993 version of the DEC Recommended Practices in the summer of 1998. A grant proposal was submitted to the U.S. Office of Special Education Programs (OSEP) for funding to support the effort. Funding was received from OSEP in the fall of 1998.

In addition to updating the practices, DEC leaders recognized the need to improve the methods for producing a set of recommended practices in order to increase the likelihood of their adoption and implementation at the child and family levels. These improved methods included (a) reviewing the research literature for practices that result in improved outcomes; (b) conducting focus groups of parents, practitioners, administrators, and scientists to ascertain their beliefs and values about practices that result in improved outcomes; (c) synthesizing these sources of information; (d) producing recommendations for "indirect" practices or supports such as personnel preparation and policy and systems change activities necessary for the implementation of recommended practices with children and families; and (e) increasing the awareness and use of the recommended practices by disseminating the practices through user-friendly products, engaging in training activities, and collaborating with partner national organizations for dissemination to key stakeholder groups such as families and administrators.

Two primary goals guided the revision of the recommended practices:

1. To produce a thoroughly supported set of recommendations for practice for teaching young children with disabilities birth through 5 and working with their families and those who serve them.

2. To increase the likelihood of the use and adoption of the recommended practices by (a) suggesting personnel preparation and policies and systems change activities necessary for improving practice at the local level, and (b) by formatting and disseminating the practices to increase their use by stakeholder groups such as families, personnel trainers, practitioners, and administrators.

Not only did these goals require a multi-method approach to producing the practices, they also involved many individuals. As noted in the acknowledgment section, the project was conducted by four investigators (Drs. McLean, Sandall, Sexton, and Smith), three methodology consultants (Drs. Snyder, Strain, and Thompson), a strand coordinator (Dr. Odom), 13 scientific strand experts (Drs. Bagnato, Bruder, Dunst, Harbin, McWilliam, Miller, Neisworth, Salisbury, Santos, Stayton, Stremel, Trivette, and Wolery), over 100 focus group participants, over 50 literature review coders, and nearly 400 field validators. In the words of David Sexton: "In short, this extremely important endeavor could not be possible without the ongoing support and participation of such a large percentage of our membership" (Sexton, 1999).

Stage One: Identifying Recommended Practices

Experience-based practices: focus groups

Four categories of focus groups were held in 1998-99 to ascertain the recommended practices that stakeholders believed are important for improved outcomes for children and families. The four categories of focus groups were (a) scientific experts by strand, (b) families, (c) administrators, and (d) practitioners.

The scientific expert focus groups were organized by nine strands and were conducted during the 1998 DEC conference in Chicago by the expert strand chairs selected for their extensive and recognized work in a particular area. The nine focus groups and strand chairs were

- Child-Focused Practices—Mark Wolery
- Cultural/Linguistic Sensitivity—Amy Santos
- Family-Based Practices—Carl Dunst and Carol Trivette
- Interdisciplinary Models—R.A. McWilliam
- Learning Environments—Mary Beth Bruder
- Personnel Development—Vicki Stayton and Patricia Miller
- Policy/Procedures—Gloria Harbin
- Systems Change/Leadership— Christine Salisbury
- Technology Applications—Kathleen Stremel

" ... this extremely important endeavor could not be possible without the ongoing support and participation of such a large percentage of our membership"
(Sexton, 1999).

The strand chairs met with the project Management Team prior to the focus groups to review the purpose of the focus groups and general procedures for each group. Definitions were discussed and agreement reached on format for stating practices. Finally, follow-up procedures and timelines were developed. The focus groups lasted approximately two hours and were audiotaped. The practices generated by the focus groups were subsequently compiled by the strand chairs and mailed to each member of the focus group for review and verification within eight weeks. When finalized, the lists of practices were then sent to the Investigators. Subsequently, at the advice of the Management Team, a strand on Assessment was added (chaired by Stephen Bagnato and John Neisworth), the Policy/Procedure strand was combined with the Systems Change strand, and the Learning Environments and Cultural/Linguistic practices were synthesized across all other strands and practices, resulting in the seven final strands of recommended practices included in this book.

The categories of stakeholders for the three additional focus groups were families, practitioners, and administrators. These stakeholder focus groups were conducted by the Investigators during the 1998 DEC conference. The focus groups were conducted using the same procedures described above. Following each focus group, one Investigator summarized the recommended practices generated by the group. This summary was then sent to each focus group member for review and verification within eight weeks. The practices from these focus groups were subsequently organized by strand: all of the recommendations from the focus group were categorized, depending on their topic, by the Investigators into the seven strands of practice (child-focused, family-based, etc.).

Research-based practices: literature review

Data-based research published in peer reviewed professional journals since 1990 was included in the literature review. Forty-eight (48) journals across disciplines were selected to be reviewed (see Table 1 on following page). First, each article abstract was reviewed to determine if the article was an empirical study of an intervention with children with disabilities, birth through 5 and/or their families or those who serve them. Second, the article was read by coders, and coding sheets were completed on each article.

Coding sheets were developed by the methodology consultants to ensure that the article was appropriately reviewed according to the type of research methodology used. A "generic" coding sheet, used uniformly across all articles, was developed that included information such as article title, authors, journal, subjects, etc. Then, a specialized coding sheet by methodology type was completed. These included coding sheets for group quantitative design, single subject design, descriptive design, qualitative design, and mixed method design. The information on the specialized coding sheets included article identification, research design features, sample, setting, outcome measures, duration of intervention, findings, recommended practices supported by the study, and "strand."

Forty-two "first stage" coders were trained, and intercoder reliability was established with the methodology consultant. These coders were assigned articles; they read each article and completed generic and specialized coding sheets for each. Twenty-nine "second stage" coders read articles that had been coded by a first stage coder and validated the recommended practice and strand placement generated by the first coder. Discrepancies were reviewed and agreement reached by the Investigators.

Table 1: Peer-Reviewed Journals Included in DEC Research Synthesis

- *American Journal on Mental Retardation*
- *Archives of Physical Medicine and Rehabilitation*
- *Augmentative and Alternative Communication*
- *Behavior Modification*
- *Behavior Therapy*
- *Behavioral Disorders*
- *Child: Care, Health & Development*
- *Child Development*
- *Developmental Medicine and Child Neurology*
- *Developmental Psychology*
- *Diagnostique*
- *Early Childhood Research Quarterly*
- *Early Education and Development*
- *Education and Training in Mental Retardation and Developmental Disabilities*
- *Education and Treatment of Children*
- *Exceptional Children*
- *Exceptionality*
- *Family Relations*
- *Infant-Toddler Intervention*
- *Infants & Young Children*
- *Journal of Abnormal Child Psychology*
- *Journal of Applied Behavior Analysis*
- *Journal of Applied Developmental Psychology*
- *Journal of Behavioral Education*
- *Journal of Communication Disorders*
- *Journal of Early Intervention*
- *Journal of Emotional and Behavioral Disorders*
- *Journal of Marriage and Family*
- *Journal of Pediatric Nursing*
- *Journal of Pediatric Psychology*
- *Journal of Special Education Technology*
- *Journal of Speech, Language, and Hearing Research*
- *Journal of Visual Impairment and Blindness*
- *Language, Speech & Hearing Services in Schools*
- *Mental Retardation*
- *Merrill-Palmer Quarterly*
- *Neonatal Network: Journal of Neonatal Nursing*
- *Pediatric Physical Therapy*
- *Pediatrics*
- *Physical & Occupational Therapy in Pediatrics*
- *Physical Therapy*
- *Teacher Education and Special Education*
- *The American Journal of Occupational Therapy*
- *The Journal of Special Education*
- *The Journal of The Association for Persons with Severe Handicaps*
- *The Occupational Therapy Journal of Research*
- *The Volta Review*
- *Topics in Early Childhood Special Education*

chapter
9

The number of articles included in the review was 1,022. Articles using each research methodology category represented the following percent of the total (1,022) articles reviewed

- Group Quantitative—52%
- Single Subject—22%
- Descriptive—13%
- Qualitative—11%
- Mixed Method—1%

After review, approximately 50 articles were removed because the research conducted did not lead to a clear practice or the study did not meet all the criteria for inclusion. This entire process generated 1,606 practices from the literature. The practices were assigned to the seven strands by the coders. As noted above, a second coder validated the practice and strand placement and the assignments were verified by the Investigators.

Stage Two: Synthesize and Syncretize Practices

The focus group and literature practices were combined (synthesized) within each strand (see Figure 1 on the following page) by the Investigators. This synthesis combined like practices, deleted duplications, and added new concepts. These lists of practices by strand were submitted to participants in several sessions at the 1999 DEC conference for review and comment and were subsequently submitted to the strand chairs and Management Team for final verification. The final number of practices after the synthesis and syncretization was 240.

Stage Three: Field Validation of Practices

The validation stage included two steps: (1) verification among experts: (a) strand leaders reviewed practices and articles and (b) the management team reviewed practices and articles in question; and, (2) performance of the field validation, described following.

The final list of 240 practices was formatted into a questionnaire for field validation. Due to the large number of practices, two forms of the questionnaire were created by assigning odd-numbered items to Form A and even-numbered items to

Figure 1: Data Collection, Analysis, and Synthesis of Recommendations From Data Sources

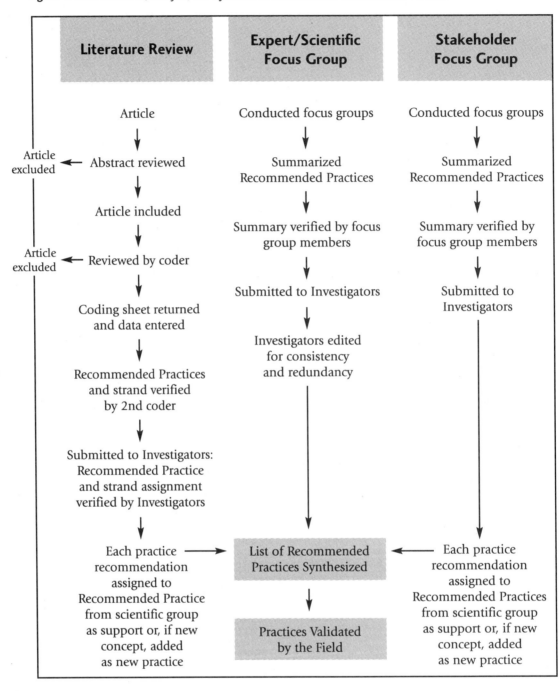

Form B. Respondents, therefore, only had to validate 120 practices each. Respondents used a Likert-type scale to rate [strongly agree (SA), agree (A), disagree (D), strongly disagree (SD), or undecided (?)] each item as to whether it was a recommended practice in Early Intervention/Early Childhood Special Education. Respondents were also asked to rate how often the practice is used [frequently (F), sometimes (S), rarely (R), never (N), or undecided (?)] in programs with which they were familiar. (See Figure 2 for an

Figure 2: Field Validation Example

	This is a recommended practice	Extent to which you see this in practice
A1. Professionals provide families with easy access by phone or other means for arranging initial screening and other activities.	SA A D SD ?	F S R N ?
Code: SA = Strongly Agree; A = Agree; D = Disagree; SD = Strongly Disagree; ? = Undecided F = Frequently; S = Sometimes; R = Rarely; N = Never; ? = Undecided		

example of an item from the field validation questionnaire.) A space for comments was also provided.

Three groups comprised the validation sample of 800 people. The first group consisted of 400 DEC members. This group was selected randomly from the DEC membership list. A second group consisted of 200 parents. This group included individuals identified by the DEC Family Consortium and also individuals randomly selected from the mailing list of members of the Federation for Children with Special Needs. The third group was comprised of 200 individuals in higher education and administrative positions in Early Intervention/Early Childhood Special Education, including individuals randomly selected from the list of Part C and 619 Coordinators from each state. All groups included volunteers who responded to requests at the annual DEC conference and to a notice in the journal *Young Exceptional Children* journal to participate in the field validation.

Questionnaires were mailed to participants. The initial mailing to respondents was followed 1 month later by a post card reminder. A second post card reminder was mailed approximately 1 month after the first. A return rate of 51% was obtained. The criterion used to determine whether a practice should be considered to be a validated recommended practice was that more than 50% of the respondents to a particular item indicated "strongly agree" or "agree" in response to the statement: "This is a recommended practice." All of the 240 practices included in Form A and Form B of the survey passed this criterion. Therefore, all of the practices were validated as recommended practices.

Stage Four: Determining Product Formats

To improve dissemination and use of the practices, four focus groups were held in 1999 to find out what formats stakeholder groups preferred for the practices. The groups were families, practitioners, administrators, and personnel trainers. Producing products in styles and formats preferred by these groups will likely increase the adoption of the practices and impact the likelihood that services will be improved. Focus groups

chapter 9

recommended products that are not overly technical, are reader friendly, and are easy to use. Second, all focus group participants recommended utilizing a variety of media including print, video, and web-based. All focus groups stressed the need for multiple formats ranging from short, awareness types of products to more in-depth, detailed products. They also suggested that products provide examples for use.

Future Activities

As a result of the format focus groups' recommendations, DEC is developing checklists, overviews, training modules, videos, and web-based materials. The literature references for the recommended practices are not included in this book because of the number of references (970). However, this reference list by strand will be available from the DEC website (www.dec-sped.org). In addition to this book, DEC has developed administrator guidelines, a self-assessment, and a parent checklist. Samples of these instruments are included in this book. We are currently field-testing the program's self-assessment procedures. We are also preparing videos and web-based products. Regional training opportunities are also being planned on the Recommended Practices to supplement annual national conference offerings. These activities are focused on the need for widespread dissemination to facilitate the goal of bridging the gap between research and practice in order to improve the quality of programs and outcomes for children and families.

Reference

Sexton, D. (1999). President's message. *Young Exceptional Children, 3*(4), 1.

Chapter 10

Using DEC's Recommended Practices

· · · · · · · · · · · ·

Mary Louise Hemmeter and Barbara J. Smith

Photo by David Naylor

DEC is committed to disseminating the DEC Recommended Practices in a variety of formats in order to address the specific needs of all relevant consumers (e.g., parents, teachers, researchers). This book represents only the first of many products (both print and non-print) that will be produced based on the Recommended Practices. This section provides initial applications of the practices for family members and professionals.

These checklists are offered as *examples* of ways that individuals or teams might use the practices to guide program development or evaluation. Readers are encouraged to design their own checklists or discussion guides that focus on their particular program development needs and concerns.

Parent Checklist

· · · · · · · · · · · · · · ·

Parents and other family members often request guidance as to what to look for or what to think about when selecting or working to improve their child's program of services and supports. For purposes of this checklist, we identified some salient practices from all the DEC Recommended Practices related to the quality of center-based programs for young children with disabilities and other special needs. In order to be included in the checklist, the practices had to be observable and easily understood. Finally, the practices were reviewed by parents and revised to incorporate terminology that would be familiar to families.

Self-Assessment: Child-Focused Interventions

· · · · · · · · · · · · · · ·

This checklist was developed simply by putting the child-focused DEC Recommended Practices into a checklist format. Individuals or teams can use the checklist to determine how they are doing when it comes to the delivery of instruction and support for children with disabilities in their programs. This checklist centers solely on child-focused interventions. It does not include practices related to assessment, teamwork, or other important aspects of early intervention/early childhood special education.

In the future, following a period of field testing, expanded versions of the self-assessment that include examples and non-examples of the practices will be available. In addition, the product will cross-reference the practices with the practices and guidelines of NAEYC and the Head Start Performance Standards. Such self-assessments will be valuable as individuals, teams, and programs strive for continuous improvement.

Administrator's Essentials

This checklist was developed in a similar manner to the self-assessment checklist described above. The recommended practices identified in the Policies, Procedures, and Systems Change strand were put into a checklist format. This checklist would be appropriate for use by a variety of individuals and agencies that have responsibility for administering and/or supervising early childhood programs including local program personnel, state departments of education, and lead agencies for infant and toddler programs.

DEC Recommended Practices in Early Intervention/Early Childhood Special Education

Parent Checklist

Mary Louise Hemmeter ● December 2000

This checklist is designed to be used by parents to aid in their selection or to help improve programs for their young child with special needs. While this checklist is based on the *DEC Recommended Practices in Early Intervention/Early Childhood Special Education* (Sandall, McLean, & Smith, 2000), it does not include all of the practices. It is meant to give parents a general overview of the program by highlighting some of the salient practices. For more information on the DEC Recommended Practices and other resources, contact DEC (see contact information at the end of this checklist). Within the checklist, the term *professional* will be used to refer to teachers, therapists, classroom assistants, and others who work with children.

How do professionals work together with families to meet the needs of the children?

❑ Teams of professionals and family members make decisions and work together.

❑ Professionals from various disciplines (e.g., physical therapy, speech therapy) teach skills to each other so that when they are working with children they can work on all of the child's goals.

❑ Services are based on the child's needs, involve the child's regular caregivers, and focus on the child's regular routines.

❑ Services are provided in ways that eliminate stress, are flexible and individualized for each child and family, and promote the well being of families.

❑ Services are sensitive and responsive to the cultural, ethnic, racial, and language preferences and backgrounds of families.

How does the program determine the strengths and needs of the child and family?

❑ Programs provide families with a primary contact person and easy ways to contact that person.

❑ Families and professionals meet together to talk about the child's strengths and needs.

❑ Professionals ask families to talk about their child's interests, abilities, and needs and demonstrate to the families that this information is critical and useful in terms of developing the child's program.

reproducible

Permission to copy not required—distribution encouraged.

❑ Professionals ask families to talk about their resources, concerns, and priorities related to their child's development.

❑ Professionals use a variety of methods for determining the child's strengths and needs (e.g., observe the child in different settings, interview the primary caregivers, test the child).

❑ Professionals test children in settings that are comfortable for the child.

❑ Professionals become familiar with the child before testing him/her.

❑ Professionals and families assess children at different times during the year to measure progress. Modifications in the child's program are made based on these ongoing findings.

❑ Professionals report assessment results to families in a way that is understandable, sensitive, and responsive to the family's concerns.

❑ Families are given time to ask questions, express concerns, or make comments about assessment findings before decisions are made about the child's program.

❑ Professionals tell families about their rights related to assessment.

What does the classroom look like (if it is a center-based program)? How is the day structured?

❑ The classroom is free of safety hazards (e.g., sharp objects, slippery rugs, hazardous materials).

❑ There are interesting materials that are appropriate to the children's ages and are adapted for the needs of children with disabilities.

❑ There are materials that represent different cultures.

❑ There are a variety of different types of activities (e.g., small group, large group, centers).

❑ Activities are structured such that children can learn through interaction with materials and other children in addition to interactions with adults.

What are the teachers and other adults doing?

❑ Professionals provide children with different levels of support depending on their needs (e.g., physically assisting a child, asking questions, providing models).

❑ Professionals use teaching strategies and adaptations that promote the child's participation in classroom activities.

❑ Professionals encourage children to help each other.

❑ Professionals provide instruction to children that target their individual goals and objectives.

❑ Professionals attempt to prevent challenging behaviors by explaining class rules, planning activities that are interesting to children, minimizing the amount of time children have to wait without having something to do, and modeling appropriate social skills.

Permission to copy not required—distribution encouraged.

❑ Professionals provide parents with information about ways they can work on their children's goals during family routines and activities.

❑ Professionals use technology (e.g., switches connected to toys, choice-making boards, computers) to help children learn new skills.

❑ Professionals select technology that is available in all of the child's environments.

What are the policies of the program, and how are they communicated to families?

❑ Families are involved in the development of program policies.

❑ Program policies ensure that families understand their rights.

❑ Program policies reflect and are sensitive to the diversity of children and families in the program.

❑ Program policies are communicated to families in ways that are understandable and clear to all families.

❑ Program policies require a family-centered approach in all phases of the child's program. Policies promote the family's active participation in all decisions about their child.

❑ Program policies promote the provision of services in naturally occurring settings and routines.

❑ Program policies ensure that the child's program is based on child and family needs.

❑ Program policies promote collaboration with other programs in terms of providing services and supporting the family's transitions between programs.

❑ Program policies ensure that families are involved in all aspects of the program (e.g., curriculum development, professional development, staff evaluation).

Reference

Sandall, S., McLean, M.E., & Smith, B.J. (2000). *DEC Recommended practices in early intervention/early childhood special education.* Longmont, CO: Sopris West.

Note

This checklist is also available free of charge from the DEC website: www.dec-sped.org

For more information on *DEC Recommended Practices in Early Intervention/Early Childhood Special Education*:

Division for Early Childhood/Council for Exceptional Children
1380 Lawrence St., Suite 650, Denver, CO 80204
Phone: (303) 556-3328 Fax: (303) 556-3310
Email: dec@ceo.cudenver.edu
Website: www.dec-sped.org

chapter

10

reproducible

To order a copy of *DEC Recommended Practices in Early Intervention/Early Childhood Special Education* contact:

Sopris West
4093 Specialty Place
Phone: (800) 547-6747 Fax: (888) 819-7767
Website: www.sopriswest.com

Disclaimer

Funding for this publication came in part from a grant to the University of Colorado at Denver and the Division for Early Childhood from the U.S. Department of Education, Office of Special Education Programs (grant no. H324D.980033). The contents of this book do not necessarily reflect the views or policies of the U.S. Department of Education or the University of Colorado at Denver.

The Division for Early Childhood assumes no liability or risk that may be incurred as a consequence, directly or indirectly, of the use and application of any of the contents of this publication. DEC does not perform due diligence on advertisers or their products or services and cannot endorse or guarantee that their offerings are suitable or accurate.

chapter
10

reproducible

Permission to copy not required—distribution encouraged.

DEC
Recommended Practices

DEC Recommended Practices in Early Intervention/Early Childhood Special Education

Self-Assessment: Child-Focused Interventions

Mary Louise Hemmeter • December 2000

This checklist centers solely on the child-focused intervention practices of the *DEC Recommended Practices in Early Intervention/Early Childhood Special Education* (Sandall, McLean, & Smith, 2000). It does not include the DEC Recommended Practices related to assessment, teamwork, or other important aspects of early intervention/early childhood special education. Professionals can use this checklist to determine how they are doing when it comes to the delivery of instruction and support for children with disabilities. Following a period of field testing, expanded versions of this self-assessment that will include examples and non-examples of the practices will be available through DEC. This product will also cross-reference the practices with the guidelines of the National Association for the Education of Young Children (NAEYC) and the Head Start Performance Standards. Such self-assessments will be valuable as individuals, teams, and programs strive for continuous improvement. Other resources to aid in implementing the practices will include videos and training opportunities.

Adults design environments to promote children's safety, active engagement, learning, participation, and membership.

❑ Learning environments meet accepted standards of quality including curriculum, child-staff ratios, group size, and physical design of the classroom.

❑ Interventionists ensure the physical and emotional safety and security of children while children are in their care.

❑ A variety of appropriate settings and naturally occurring activities are used to facilitate children's learning and development.

❑ Services are provided in natural learning environments as appropriate. These include places where typical children participate, such as home or community settings.

❑ Physical space and materials are structured and adapted to promote engagement, play, interaction, and learning by attending to children's preferences and interests, using novelty, using responsive toys, providing adequate amounts of materials, and using defined spaces.

❑ The social environment is structured to promote engagement, interaction, communication, and learning by providing peer models, peer proximity, responsive adults, imitative adults, and expanding children's play and behavior.

reproducible

❑ Routines and transitions are structured to promote interaction, communication, and learning by being responsive to child behavior, using naturalistic time delay, interrupted chain procedure, transition-based teaching, and visual cue systems.

❑ Play routines are structured to promote interaction, communication, and learning by defining roles for dramatic play, prompting engagement, group friendship activities, and using specialized props.

❑ Environments are designed and activities are conducted so that children learn about or are exposed to multiple cultures and languages by, among other practices, allowing children and families to share their cultures and languages with others, to the extent they desire.

❑ Interventionists facilitate children's engagement with their environment to encourage child-initiated learning that is not dependent on the adult's presence.

❑ Adults provide environments that foster positive relationships including peer-peer, parent/caregiver-child, and parent-caregiver relationships.

Adults individualize and adapt practices for each child based on ongoing data to meet children's changing needs.

❑ Practices and goals are individualized for each child based on: (a) the child's current behavior and abilities across relevant domains instead of the child's diagnostic category; (b) the family's view of what the child needs to learn; (c) interventionist and specialist views of what the child needs to learn; and (d) the demands, expectations, and requirements of the child's current environments.

❑ Practices target meaningful outcomes for the child that build upon the child's current skills and behaviors and promote membership with others.

❑ Data-based decisions are used to make modifications in practices. Child performance is monitored and data are collected to determine the impact of the practices on the child's progress and to make modifications in the intervention if needed. The ongoing monitoring must be feasible and useful within the child's environment.

❑ Recommended practices are used to teach/promote whatever skills are necessary for children to function more completely, competently, adaptively, and independently in the child's natural environments. These skills should be those that maximize participation and membership in home, school, and community environments, including those that are typical or similar to other persons' in those environments. Attention should be given to the breadth and sophistication of the child's skills.

❑ Children's behavior is recognized, interpreted in context, responded to contingently, and opportunities are provided for expansion or elaboration of child behavior by imitating the behavior, waiting for the child's responses, modeling, and prompting.

chapter
10

reproducible

Adults use systematic procedures within and across environments, activities, and routines to promote children's learning and participation.

❑ Interventionists are agents of change to promote and accelerate learning, and that learning should be viewed in different phases (i.e., acquisition, fluency, maintenance, generalization) that require different types of practices.

❑ Practices are used systematically, frequently, and consistently within and across environments (e.g., home, center, community) and across people (i.e., those who care for and interact regularly with the child).

❑ Planning that considers the situation (e.g., class, home, etc.) in which the intervention will be applied occurs prior to implementation.

❑ Practices that are used are validated, normalized, useful across environments, respectful, and not stigmatizing of the child and family and are sensitive to linguistic and cultural issues.

❑ Systematic naturalistic teaching procedures such as models, expansions, incidental teaching, mand model, and naturalistic time delay are used to promote acquisition and use of communication and social skills.

❑ Peer-mediated strategies are used to promote social and communicative behavior.

❑ Prompting and fading procedures (e.g., modeling, graduated guidance, increasing assistance, time delay) are used to ensure acquisition and use of communicative, self-care, cognitive, and social skills.

❑ Instructional strategies such as those described above are embedded and distributed within and across activities.

❑ Recommended instructional strategies are used with sufficient fidelity, consistency, frequency, and intensity to ensure high levels of behavior occurring frequently.

❑ Consequences for children's behavior are structured to increase the complexity and duration of children's play, engagement, appropriate behavior, and learning by using differential reinforcement, response shaping, high-probability procedures (i.e., behavioral momentum), and correspondence training.

❑ For problem behaviors, interventionists should assess the behavior in context to identify its function, and then devise interventions that are comprehensive in that they make the behavior irrelevant (i.e., the child's environment is modified so that problem behavior is unnecessary or precluded), inefficient (i.e., a more efficient replacement behavior is taught), and ineffective (i.e., reinforcement and other consequent events are used).

Reference

Sandall, S., McLean, M.E., & Smith, B.J. (2000). *DEC Recommended practices in early intervention/early childhood special education.* Longmont, CO: Sopris West.

Note

This checklist is also available free of charge from the DEC website: www.dec-sped.org

For more information on *DEC Recommended Practices in Early Intervention/Early Childhood Special Education*:

Division for Early Childhood/Council for Exceptional Children
1380 Lawrence St., Suite 650, Denver, CO 80204
Phone: (303) 556-3328 Fax: (303) 556-3310
Email: dec@ceo.cudenver.edu
Website: www.dec-sped.org

To order a copy of *DEC Recommended Practices in Early Intervention/Early Childhood Special Education* contact:

Sopris West
4093 Specialty Place
Phone: (800) 547-6747 Fax: (888) 819-7767
Website: www.sopriswest.com

Disclaimer

Funding for this publication came in part from a grant to the University of Colorado at Denver and the Division for Early Childhood from the U.S. Department of Education, Office of Special Education Programs (grant no. H324D.980033). The contents of this book do not necessarily reflect the views or policies of the U.S. Department of Education or the University of Colorado at Denver.

The Division for Early Childhood assumes no liability or risk that may be incurred as a consequence, directly or indirectly, of the use and application of any of the contents of this publication. DEC does not perform due diligence on advertisers or their products or services and cannot endorse or guarantee that their offerings are suitable or accurate.

chapter
10

reproducible

Permission to copy not required—distribution encouraged.

DEC Recommended Practices in Early Intervention/Early Childhood Special Education

Administrator's Essentials:

Creating Policies and Procedures That Support Recommended Practices in Early Intervention/Early Childhood Special Education (EI/ECSE)

Barbara J. Smith ● December 2000

There is a link between program quality and child outcomes. Therefore, programs that employ best practices will positively impact the outcomes of children and families they serve.

Implementing recommended practices in services for young children with disabilities and their families requires administrative policies, procedures, and structures that will support such practice. For instance, providing family-based resources and supports or child-focused services in natural settings requires flexible personnel job descriptions and hours of work that promote service provision in the home or community setting during hours convenient for the family or community program. Recommended practices also require cutting-edge knowledge and skills through on-going, job-related training and technical assistance supports. This richness of policies, procedures, and supports will occur only if administrators (a) are knowledgeable of recommended practice in EI/ECSE, (b) share resources with other programs and agencies, and (c) engage in systems change and planning.

This checklist contains relevant recommended practices from the seven strands of the *DEC Recommended Practices in Early Intervention/Early Childhood Special Education* (Sandall, McLean, & Smith, 2000) that give specific direction to administrators. Most of these recommendations are found in the Policies, Procedures, and Systems Change chapter of the DEC Recommended Practices. This checklist of selected practices can be used by administrators to reflect on their policies. However, administrators are encouraged to become familiar with all of the practices in *DEC Recommended Practices in Early Intervention/Early Childhood Special Education* (Sandall, McLean, & Smith, 2000) in order to appropriately serve young children with disabilities and their families.

reproducible

Administrators, other professionals, and families shape policy at the national, state, and local levels that promote the use of recommended practices in early intervention/early childhood special education.

Examples/Notes:

Is this practice evident in policy/procedure?   ❑ Yes   ❑ Emerging   ❑ No

Administrators ensure that they and their staff have the knowledge, training, and credentials necessary to implement the DEC Recommended Practices in early intervention/early childhood special education.

- Program coordinators/supervisors have training in early childhood education, early intervention, early childhood special education, and supervision.

  Examples/Notes:

  Is this practice evident in policy/procedure?   ❑ Yes   ❑ Emerging   ❑ No

- Administrators are affiliated with professional early childhood/early childhood special education organizations and encourage staff to maintain their affiliations. Continuing education such as staff attendance at meetings and conferences to enhance professional growth is supported.

  Examples/Notes:

  Is this practice evident in policy/procedure?   ❑ Yes   ❑ Emerging   ❑ No

- Program policies provide clear job descriptions and provide for personnel competencies and on-going staff development, technical assistance, supervision, and evaluation to inform and improve the skills of practitioners and administrators.

  Examples/Notes:

  Is this practice evident in policy/procedure?   ❑ Yes   ❑ Emerging   ❑ No

chapter 10

reproducible

Permission to copy not required—distribution encouraged.

Program policies and administration promote families as partners in the planning and delivery of services, supports, and resources.

- When creating program policies and procedures, strategies are employed to capture family and community voices and to support the active and meaningful participation of families and community groups including those that are traditionally underrepresented.

  Examples/Notes:

  Is this practice evident in policy/procedure? ❏ Yes ❏ Emerging ❏ No

- Program policies create a participatory decision-making process of all stakeholders including individuals with disabilities. Training in teaming is provided as needed.

  Examples/Notes:

  Is this practice evident in policy/procedure? ❏ Yes ❏ Emerging ❏ No

- Program policies ensure that families understand their rights including conflict resolution, confidentiality, and other matters.

  Examples/Notes:

  Is this practice evident in policy/procedure? ❏ Yes ❏ Emerging ❏ No

- Program policies are examined and revised as needed to ensure that they reflect and respect the diversity of children, families, and personnel.

  Examples/Notes:

  Is this practice evident in policy/procedure? ❏ Yes ❏ Emerging ❏ No

chapter
10

reproducible

Permission to copy not required—distribution encouraged.

• Program policies are provided in sufficient detail and formats so that all stakeholders understand what the policy means.

Examples/Notes:

Is this practice evident in policy/procedure?   ❑ Yes   ❑ Emerging   ❑ No

• Program policies require a family-centered approach in all decisions and phases of service delivery (system entry, assessment procedures, Individualized Family Service Plan (IFSP)/Individualized Education Program (IEP), intervention, transition, etc.) including presenting families with flexible and individualized options for the location, timing, and types of services, supports, and resources that are not disruptive of family life.

Examples/Notes:

Is this practice evident in policy/procedure?   ❑ Yes   ❑ Emerging   ❑ No

• Program policies provide for the dissemination of information about program initiatives and outcomes to stakeholders.

Examples/Notes:

Is this practice evident in policy/procedure?   ❑ Yes   ❑ Emerging   ❑ No

Program policies and administration promote the use of DEC's and other recommended practices.

• Program policies reflect recommended practices including personnel standards, child-staff ratios, group size, case loads, safety, assistive technology, and EI/ECSE services and practices. Incentives, training, and technical assistance to promote the use of recommended practices in all settings are provided.

Examples/Notes:

Is this practice evident in policy/procedure?   ❑ Yes   ❑ Emerging   ❑ No

- Program policies establish accountability systems that provide resources, supports, and clear action steps to ensure compliance with regulations and to ensure that recommended practices are adopted, utilized, maintained, and evaluated resulting in high quality services.

  Examples/Notes:

  Is this practice evident in policy/procedure? ❑ Yes ❑ Emerging ❑ No

- Program policies support the provision of services in inclusive or natural learning environments (places in which typical children participate such as the home or community settings, public and private preschools, child care, recreation groups, etc.). Strategies are used to overcome challenges to inclusion.

  Examples/Notes:

  Is this practice evident in policy/procedure? ❑ Yes ❑ Emerging ❑ No

- Program policies ensure that the IFSP/IEP is used on a regular and frequent basis to determine the type and amounts of services, the location of services and desired outcomes.

  Examples/Notes:

  Is this practice evident in policy/procedure? ❑ Yes ❑ Emerging ❑ No

- Program policies ensure that family supports, service coordination, transitions, and other practices occur in response to child and family needs rather than being determined by the age of the child (e.g., b-2, 3-5).

  Examples/Notes:

  Is this practice evident in policy/procedure? ❑ Yes ❑ Emerging ❑ No

chapter
10

reproducible

- Program policies ensure that multiple instructional models are available to meet the individual needs of children (e.g., less structure to more structure; child-driven to teacher-driven; peer-mediated to teacher-mediated, etc.).

  Examples/Notes:

  Is this practice evident in policy/procedure? ❑ Yes   ❑ Emerging   ❑ No

- Administrators provide for a supportive work environment (e.g., hiring and retention policies, compensation and benefits, safety, workspace, etc.).

  Examples/Notes:

  Is this practice evident in policy/procedure? ❑ Yes   ❑ Emerging   ❑ No

Program policies and administration promote interagency and interdisciplinary collaboration.

- Program policies include structures and mechanisms such as job descriptions, planning time, training, and resources for teaming resulting in meaningful participation for on-going coordination among professionals, families, and programs related to service delivery including transition.

  Examples/Notes:

  Is this practice evident in policy/procedure? ❑ Yes   ❑ Emerging   ❑ No

- Program policies facilitate and provide for comprehensive and coordinated systems of services through interagency collaboration by clearly delineating the components, activities, and responsibilities of all agencies (e.g., joint policies across agencies; collaborative planning on a system, child, and family basis; shared forms and plans; etc.).

  Examples/Notes:

  Is this practice evident in policy/procedure? ❑ Yes   ❑ Emerging   ❑ No

chapter 10

reproducible

- Program policies result in families and professionals from different disciplines working as a team developing and implementing IFSPs/IEPs that integrate their expertise into common goals.

  Examples/Notes:

  Is this practice evident in policy/procedure? ❑ Yes ❑ Emerging ❑ No

Program policies, administration, and leadership promote program evaluation and systems change efforts at the community level.

- A shared vision (of all stakeholders), clear values/beliefs, and an understanding of the culture and context to be changed guide efforts to restructure and reform systems. Decisions about what to change result from regular analysis and evaluation of discrepancies among the vision, beliefs, knowledge, and current practices.

  Examples/Notes:

  Is this practice evident in policy/procedure? ❑ Yes ❑ Emerging ❑ No

- Assessment of the interests, issues, and priorities of constituent groups guides the selection and direction of leadership and systems change strategies.

  Examples/Notes:

  Is this practice evident in policy/procedure? ❑ Yes ❑ Emerging ❑ No

- Leadership and systems change efforts produce positive outcomes for children, families, and communities that are responsive to their needs. Evaluation data are used to ensure: (a) service utilization, (b) more efficient and effective supports for children, families, and staff, and (c) appropriate systems change leadership and strategies.

  Examples/Notes:

  Is this practice evident in policy/procedure? ❑ Yes ❑ Emerging ❑ No

chapter
10

reproducible

Permission to copy not required—distribution encouraged.

- Leadership capacity, risk taking, and shared decision-making among professionals and families at all levels of the organization are cultivated.

  Examples/Notes:

  Is this practice evident in policy/procedure? ❑ Yes ❑ Emerging ❑ No

- Leadership and systems change efforts include attention to: timely job-embedded professional development, funding, program evaluation, accountability, governance, program accreditation, curriculum and naturalistic instruction/supports.

  Examples/Notes:

  Is this practice evident in policy/procedure? ❑ Yes ❑ Emerging ❑ No

- Leadership and systems change efforts rely on strong relationships and collaboration within and across systems: between consumer and system, across systems that deal with children and families, among components within a system, and among professionals from diverse disciplines.

  Examples/Notes:

  Is this practice evident in policy/procedure? ❑ Yes ❑ Emerging ❑ No

- Leadership is committed and willing to change organizational structures (staffing, schedules, teaming) to be responsive to individual needs.

  Examples/Notes:

  Is this practice evident in policy/procedure? ❑ Yes ❑ Emerging ❑ No

chapter

10

reproducible

Permission to copy not required—distribution encouraged.

- Change is institutionalized through the development of coordinated management and accountability systems.

  Examples/Notes:

  Is this practice evident in policy/procedure?   ❑ Yes   ❑ Emerging   ❑ No

- Resources are provided for program evaluation that occurs along established time points, incorporating appropriate measurable indicators of progress including child and family outcomes and preferences.

  Examples/Notes:

  Is this practice evident in policy/procedure?   ❑ Yes   ❑ Emerging   ❑ No

- Program evaluation is comprehensive, is multi-dimensional, and incorporates a variety of methods for assessing the progress and outcomes of change. Evaluation efforts take into account differing cultural, contextual, demographic, and experiential perspectives including those of parents and of individuals with disabilities.

  Examples/Notes:

  Is this practice evident in policy/procedure?   ❑ Yes   ❑ Emerging   ❑ No

- Program policies delineate all components of service delivery and provide for tracking and evaluation of all components, including child and family outcomes, to ensure that recommended practices are implemented as intended.

  Examples/Notes:

  Is this practice evident in policy/procedure?   ❑ Yes   ❑ Emerging   ❑ No

chapter
10

reproducible

Permission to copy not required—distribution encouraged.

Reference

Sandall, S., McLean, M.E., & Smith, B.J. (2000). *DEC Recommended practices in early intervention/early childhood special education.* Longmont, CO: Sopris West.

Note

This checklist is also available free of charge from the DEC website: www.dec-sped.org

For more information on *DEC Recommended Practices in Early Intervention/Early Childhood Special Education*:

Division for Early Childhood/Council for Exceptional Children
1380 Lawrence St., Suite 650, Denver, CO 80204
Phone: (303) 556-3328 Fax: (303) 556-3310
Email: dec@ceo.cudenver.edu
Website: www.dec-sped.org

To order a copy of *DEC Recommended Practices in Early Intervention/Early Childhood Special Education* contact:

Sopris West
4093 Specialty Place
Phone: (800) 547-6747 Fax: (888) 819-7767
Website: www.sopriswest.com

Disclaimer

Funding for this publication came in part from a grant to the University of Colorado at Denver and the Division for Early Childhood from the U.S. Department of Education, Office of Special Education Programs (grant no. H324D.980033). The contents of this book do not necessarily reflect the views or policies of the U.S. Department of Education or the University of Colorado at Denver.

The Division for Early Childhood assumes no liability or risk that may be incurred as a consequence, directly or indirectly, of the use and application of any of the contents of this publication. DEC does not perform due diligence on advertisers or their products or services and cannot endorse or guarantee that their offerings are suitable or accurate.

chapter
10

reproducible

Chapter 11

Concluding Thoughts

· · · · · · · · · · ·

Photo by David Naylor

Susan Sandall, Mary E. McLean, and Barbara J. Smith

The purpose of this book is to provide guidance to families and program personnel as they select, develop, implement, and evaluate services and supports for young children with disabilities and their families. In addition, the practices offer useful guidelines for those who prepare the personnel who design and offer services and supports. The impact those individuals (teachers, therapists, service coordinators) have on families' lives is tremendous. In our focus groups, parents often shared stories about such individuals. "I'll never forget her," one mother said. One parent described her child's first home visitor by saying, " . . . that was the biggest gift." Families also told us how important it was that these individuals be knowledgeable and work together with them.

Our aim in this book is to share the knowledge gained from the integration of the scientific literature with the experience and knowledge of researchers, parents, practitioners, administrators, and personnel trainers. This project has been a self-examination, undertaken by the field, of quality in early intervention/early childhood special education. The process was driven by our conviction that there is a link between high-quality programs and positive outcomes for children and families. The practices that emerged from this process when implemented in programs will, we believe, lead to improved child development and learning and enhanced family functioning.

· · · · · · · · · · ·

The impact those individuals (teachers, therapists, service coordinators) have on families' lives is tremendous.

· · · · · · · · · · ·

The DEC Recommended Practices are important. Yet, we know that they will continue to change as the field and society change. A professional organization must periodically examine the established practices in its professional discipline. With the participation of many, many DEC members and other colleagues we have undertaken the examination.

Where do we go from here? Our analysis of the themes, practices, and findings derived from the literature and the focus groups will continue. Throughout this book we've described the myriad plans for future products and training activities. Our efforts will focus on dissemination, training, and systems change to meet the promise of high quality programs for young children with disabilities and their families.

Janice Fialka uses the metaphor of the dance to talk about the time, energy, candor, and commitment that are necessary in early intervention/early childhood special education.

> *I believe that if parents and professionals are to be effective in creating marvelous opportunities for our children, then both sets of partners must carve out time to get to know each other's dreams, hopes, fears, constraints, and perspectives. We must take off our own sets of headphones and be willing to hear each other's music, with special attention to and inclusion of the parent's music and unique dance steps. To truly get to know the child, we must also get to know each other, not just as parents and professionals, but as people, too. This is hard work and takes patience, trust, and lots of getting to know each other. It is one of the most significant ways we can make a difference in the lives of our children (Fialka, 2000).*

To truly get to know the child, we must also get to know each other, not just as parents and professionals, but as people, too.

Reference

Fialka, J. (2000). The dance of partnership: Why do my feet hurt? *Young Exceptional Children, 4*(1).

chapter

11

Appendices

● ● ● ● ● ●

Appendix A

Additional Acknowledgments

. . . .

Literature Coders and Validators
. . . .

Melinda Ault
Meher Banajee
Cindy Bernheimer
Ted Bovey
Bill Brown
Debbie Bruns
P. Kay Nottingham Chaplin
Hsin-Ying Chou
Martha Cook
Leslie Craig-Unkerfer
Sharon Darling
Beth Delaney
Karen Diamond
Cyndi DiCarlo
Glen Dunlap
Sayaka Endo
Dennis Fell
Linda Flynn
Peggy Gallagher
Michael Gamel-McCormick
Mary Francis Hanline
Kathryn Haring
Mary Louise Hemmeter
Debra Reichert Hoge
Eva Horn
Mark Innocenti
Hazel Jones
Debra Judd
Michael Kelley
Jennifer Kilgo

Frank Kohler
Susan Kontos
Maggie LaMontagne
Karen La Paro
Antoinette Jardine Ledet
David Lovett
Bonnie McBride
Jeanette McCollum
Mary E. McLean
Leslie Munson
Samuel L. Odom
Melissa Olive
Jeff Oremland
Richard Roberts
Beth Rous
Diane Sainato
Susan Sandall
John Schuster
Ilene Schwartz
David Sexton
M'Lisa Shelden
Steve Stile
Phillip S. Strain
Bruce Thompson
Carole Torrey
Laura Vagianos
Margaret Werts
Ruth Wolery
Paul Yoder

Focus Groups

Members of Scientific Focus Groups

Members of these focus groups generated recommendations within a particular strand of practices. They are also listed within the strand chapters they worked on.

Lynette Aytch

Isaura Barrera

Gwen Beegle

Harriet Boone

Barbara Bowman

Darbi Breath

Pip Campbell

Michael Conn-Powers

Vivian Correa

Juliann Woods Cripe

Laurie Dinnebeil

Marilyn Espe-Sherwindt

Susan Fowler

Lise Fox

Jim Gallagher

Corrine Garland

Howard Goldstein

Lourdes Gonzalez

Ann Hains

Marci Hanson

Eva Horn

Mark Innocenti

Leslie Jackson

George Jesien

Joan Karp

Louise Kaczmarek

John Killoran

Diana LaRocco

Esther Leung

Gerry Mahoney

Jeanette McCollum

Penny Milburn

Richard Roberts

Sharon Rosenkoetter

Sarah Rule

Diane Sainato

Barbara Schwartz

Daphne Thomas

Carol M. Trivette

Sharon Walsh

Amy Whitehead

Barbara Wolfe

Members of Stakeholder Focus Groups on Practices

Members of these focus groups represented family members, practitioners, and administrators and discussed and made recommendations related to practices across all strands.

Linda Brault

Darbi Breath

Mary Jane Brotherson

Cyndi DiCarlo

Amy Hicks

Ellen Hunt-Landry

Sharon Kilpatrick

Andrea Knowlton

Jenny Lange

Diana LaRocco

Faye Manaster Eldar

Bonnie McBride

Donna Miller

Lorna Mullis

Bruce Orr

Mike Plotzker

Karen Sullivan

Beth Swedeen

Judy Swett

Deb Ziegler

appendix

A

Members of Stakeholder Focus Groups on Format

Members of these focus groups represented family members, practitioners, administrators, and personnel trainers and discussed and recommended best formats for the use and adoption of the DEC Recommended Practices.

Jane Amundson
Mako Arai
Ellen Browning
Patricia Caro
Paula Caston
Camille Catlett
Renee Charlifue-Smith
Terry DeLeonardis
Corrine Donley
Stephanie Frazier
Ann Hains
Kathy Hart
Joe Hauth
Marian Hauth
Lauren Heller Kerstein
Maureen Huguley
Lucinda Hundley

Tracy Jirikowic
Gail Joseph
Maureen Kelly
Rita Lee
Desire Loeb-Guth
Julie Mack
Mary Ann Marchel
Julie Newman
Linda O'Neil
Mele Olsen
Amy Phillpott
Ann Riall
Helen Richards
Linda Tuchman
Lizzie Waterson
Fran Wegener
Amy Whitehead

appendix A

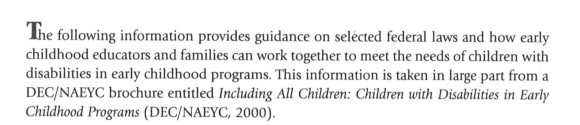

Appendix B

Selected Federal Laws and Resources Related to Children with Disabilities in Early Childhood Programs

· · · · · · · · · · · ·

The following information provides guidance on selected federal laws and how early childhood educators and families can work together to meet the needs of children with disabilities in early childhood programs. This information is taken in large part from a DEC/NAEYC brochure entitled *Including All Children: Children with Disabilities in Early Childhood Programs* (DEC/NAEYC, 2000).

What disability related federal laws are important to meeting the needs of young children with disabilities?

· · · · · · · · · · · · · · · · ·

There are three important federal disability laws that relate to early care and education for young children with disabilities. These laws promote inclusion to the fullest extent and civil rights for individuals with disabilities. These laws are:

The Americans With Disabilities Act (ADA): a federal civil rights law that prohibits discrimination against people who have disabilities. The Act states that people with disabilities are entitled to equal rights in employment, state and local public services, and public accommodations such as schools and early childhood programs, including child care centers, Head Start programs, and family child care homes.

Section 504 of the Rehabilitation Act: prohibits the discrimination against children and adults on the basis of a disability by any program or activity receiving federal financial assistance. This includes any public or private preschool, child care center, Head Start/Early Head Start, or family child care home that receives federal funds either directly or through a grant, loan, or contract.

The Individuals with Disabilities Education Act (IDEA): requires states to provide early intervention and a free appropriate public education (FAPE) to eligible children with disabilities. The 1997 revisions to the Act strengthened early childhood services. There are three major provisions that apply to early childhood:

- Part C provides all states with grants for early intervention services for children from birth to age 3 (and their families) who are developmentally delayed, or at a substantial risk of delay, due to diagnosed factors and conditions. Each family and child identified receives services under a written Individualized Family Service Plan (IFSP).

- Part B requires that a free appropriate public education be available for children with disabilities ages 3–21 years. Each eligible child receives services under a written Individualized Education Program (IEP).

- Section 619 of Part B authorizes grants to all states for services for children with disabilities ages 3–5 and for continuity of special education services for children moving out of Part C.

All three of these laws encourage the inclusion of children with disabilities in all early childhood settings. These laws can assist professionals in their continuing efforts to meet the individual needs of each child and family.

What should early childhood educators do to ensure that programs are meeting ADA, Section 504, and IDEA requirements?

For ADA and Section 504, assess your program's accessibility, policies, activities, and materials. Develop action plans to:

- Evaluate your recruitment, enrollment, and employment policies and procedures to make sure they are non-discriminatory.

- Assess the physical accessibility of your setting. Rearranging furniture or installing a ramp or a handrail may be all that is required.

- Schedule time for staff to meet to develop ways your program can prepare to include children with disabilities and to evaluate their progress in meeting their needs.

- Look for other ways to accommodate children, staff, and families with disabilities in your setting.

For IDEA requirements, make sure you are following the activities and strategies of the Individualized Family Service Plan (IFSP) for infants and their families and the Individualized Education Program (IEP) for older children. Also, if you think a child in your care may have a disability or special need, you should talk with the family and provide them with contact information for your local school district or early intervention program for an IDEA evaluation.

appendix
B

Young children with disabilities who are eligible under IDEA have a right to services to meet their individual needs. Depending on the child's age, and your state's procedures, either the early intervention program or your local school district should respond to the parent's referral for evaluation. If the child is found eligible for IDEA services, an individualized plan will be developed with the child's parent(s) and others to determine what services will be provided and where they will be delivered. If you are not involved in the development of the plan, ask for a copy and for training, if needed, to implement it.

How can early childhood educators work effectively with families?

Communication with the child's family is paramount. Find out what concerns they may have about their child's development as well as what the child is able to do in their own home setting. Make sure they understand the concerns you have about their child's development as well as the child's strengths.

As a person who spends time with the child, you are in an ideal position to assist the child and family in developing goals and plans to achieve those goals. Your involvement in this process is very important!

Where can I get help?

You are not alone. There is help available.

1. Ask the families—parents know their child better than anyone and are already familiar with many resources of both services and support.
2. Ask your provider network—many providers have experience in including children with disabilities.
3. Contact your local child care resource and referral program.
4. Contact your local school district and local early intervention program. They will likely know about training and technical assistance resources.
5. Contact state/local organizations whose members provide services to children with disabilities.

For more information:

ADA Information Line
U.S. Department of Justice
Phone: 800-514-0301
TDD: 800-514-0383
Website:
www.usdoj.gov/crt.ada/adahom1.htm

The Arc of the United States
1010 Wayne Ave., Suite 650
Silver Spring, MD 20910
Phone: 800-433-5255
 or 301-565-3842
Fax: 301-565-5342
Website: www.thearc.org
E-mail: info@thearc.org

appendix
B

Architectural and Transportation Barriers Compliance Board (Access Board)
Phone: 800-872-2253
        or 202-272-5434
Fax: 202-272-5447
TDD: 800-993-2822 or 202-272-5449
Website: www.access-board.gov

Child Care Law Center
973 Market Street, Suite 550
San Francisco, CA 94103
Phone: 415-495-5498
Fax: 415-495-6734
Website: www.childcarelaw.org

IDEA Partnerships—ASPIIRE and ILIAD
[Associations of Service Providers
        Implementing IDEA Reform
        in Education (ASPIIRE) and
        IDEA Implementation by
        Local Administrators (ILIAD)]
Council for Exceptional Children
1920 Association Drive
Reston, VA 20191-1589
Phone: 877-CEC-IDEA
TDD: 703-264-9480
Website: www.ideapractices.org

National Early Childhood Technical Assistance System (NECTAS)
137 East Franklin Street, Suite 500
Chapel Hill, NC 27514
Phone: 919-962-2001
TDD: 919-962-8300
Fax: 919-966-7463
Website: www.nectas.unc.edu

National Information Center for Children and Youth with Disabilities (NICHCY)
P.O. Box 1492
Washington, DC 20013-1492
Phone: 800-695-0285
        or 202-884-8400 (Voice/TTY)
Fax: 202-884-8441
Website: www.nichcy.org
E-mail: nichcy@aed.org

Office of Special Education Program (OSEP)
U.S. Department of Education's Office
        of Special Education and
        Rehabilitative Services (OSERS)
330 C Street, SW
Mary E. Switzer Building
Washington, DC 20202
Website: www.ed.gov/offices/OSERS

National Head Start Association
1651 Prince Street
Alexandria, VA 22314
Phone: 703-739-0875
Fax: 703-739-0878
Website: www.nhsa.org

Head Start Bureau
The Administration on Children,
        Youth, and Families
U.S. Department of Health
        and Human Services
200 Independence Avenue SW
Washington, DC 20201
Phone: 877-696-6775
Website:
www2.acf.dhhs.gov/programs/hsb

appendix
B

Rehabilitation Engineering and Assistive Technology Society of North America (RESNA)

1700 North Moore Street, Suite 1540
Arlington, VA 22209-1903
Phone: 703-524-6686
FAX: 703-524-6630
TTY: 703-524-6639
Website: www.resna.org
E-mail: info@resna.org

The Division for Early Childhood (DEC) of the Council for Exceptional Children (CEC)

1380 Lawrence Street, Suite 650
Denver, CO 80204
Phone: 303-556-3328
FAX: 303-556-3310
Website: www.dec-sped.org
E-mail: dec@ceo.cudenver.edu

National Association for the Education of Young Children (NAEYC)

1509 16th Street, NW
Washington, DC 20036-1426
Phone: 800-424-2460
　　or 202-232-8777
Website: www.naeyc.org
E-mail: naeyc@naeyc.org

Reference

Division for Early Childhood (DEC) and National Association for the Education of Young Children (NAEYC). (2000). *Including all children: Children with disabilities in early childhood programs* [Brochure]. Washington, DC: National Association for the Education of Young Children (NAEYC).

To order the brochure, please contact NAEYC. Single copies are 50 cents each; 100 copies are $12. NAEYC Order #514.

appendix

B

Appendix C

DEC Positions and Concept Papers

. . . .

DEC develops and disseminates positions and concept papers on issues of importance to the field. The development of positions and concept papers involves (a) a determination by the DEC Executive Board that the field would benefit from a DEC position and/or guidance on an issue, (b) input from members on a draft statement and (c) final paper disseminated to the field as well as used by the organization for guidance in future activities.

This Appendix includes the following

1. DEC Position on Inclusion

2. DEC Position on Services for Children Birth to Age 8 with Special Needs and Their Families

3. DEC Postion on Interviews for Challenging Behavior

4. DEC Concept Paper on the Identification of and Intervention With Challenging Behavior

5. DEC Code of Ethics

THE DIVISION FOR EARLY CHILDHOOD

Division for Early Childhood (DEC) Position on Inclusion

ADOPTED: April, 1993
Revised: December, 1993
Reaffirmed: 1996
Updated: 2000

Inclusion, as a value, supports the right of all children, regardless of abilities, to participate actively in natural settings within their communities. Natural settings are those in which the child would spend time had he or she not had a disability. These settings include, but are not limited to home, preschool, nursery schools, Head Start programs, kindergartens, neighborhood school classrooms, child care, places of worship, recreational (such as community playgrounds and community events), and other settings that all children and families enjoy.

DEC supports and advocates that young children and their families have full and successful access to health, social, educational, and other support services that promote full participation in family and community life. DEC values the cultural, economic, and educational diversity of families and supports a family-guided process for identifying a program of service.

As young children participate in group settings (such as preschool, play groups, child care, kindergarten) their active participation should be guided by developmentally and individually appropriate curriculum. Access to and participation in the age appropriate general curriculum becomes central to the identification and provision of specialized support services.

To implement inclusive practices DEC supports: (a) the continued development, implementation, evaluation, and dissemination of full inclusion supports, services, and systems that are of high quality for all children; (b) the development of preservice and inservice training programs that prepare families, service providers, and administrators to develop and work within inclusive settings; (c) collaboration among key stakeholders to implement flexible fiscal and administrative procedures in support of inclusion; (d) research that contributes to our knowledge of recommended practice; and (e) the restructuring and unification of social, educational, health, and intervention supports and services to make them more responsive to the needs of all children and families. Ultimately, the implementation of inclusive practice must lead to optimal developmental benefit for each individual child and family.

Endorsed by NAEYC—April 1994, April 1998

. . . .

Permission to copy not required—distribution encouraged.

 THE DIVISION FOR EARLY CHILDHOOD

Division for Early Childhood (DEC) Position on Services for Children Birth to Age 8 With Special Needs and Their Families

ADOPTED: December, 1993
REVISED: July 21, 1998

DEC strongly supports and encourages the identification and delivery of comprehensive and coordinated supports and services to children with special needs and their families as early as possible, in accordance with the priorities of their families. Young children with special needs are those between birth and age 8 who have disabilities, developmental delays, are at-risk for future developmental problems, or who are gifted and talented.

This position is based on the following beliefs: (1) all young children are valued and full participants in their families, communities, and schools; (2) high quality early intervention can help ensure that all young children reach their full developmental potential and attain functional skills in the areas of communication, mobility, social competence, cognition, and self care; and, (3) families benefit from consistent and supportive partnerships and collaborations with service providers such as early childhood special educators, early childhood educators, related service personnel, child care providers, and others who provide supports and services to their children. This position is derived from: the professional literature, which provides ample research evidence for the efficacy of early intervention for young children with special needs and their families; parental leadership and collaborations across the country; and federal, state, and provincial policies that encourage and support early intervention and early childhood special education services.

DEC proposes that all young children with special needs are entitled to early intervention services that reflect recommended practices as presented in the literature and the *DEC Recommended Practices* (1993). These practices emphasize the individualized nature of service delivery as determined collaboratively by families and professionals through the Individualized Family Service Plan (IFSP) or Individualized Education Program (IEP) process. This process guarantees each child a comprehensive assessment to identify individual strengths and needs; appropriate intervention at the intensity and scope warranted by the child's etiology and developmental profile; research and best practice related to these variables; and family preference. Further, the IFSP or IEP process should monitor child progress to ensure service modifications as needed.

All children in need of early intervention or early childhood special education should be able to attain basic skills in the areas of communication, mobility, cognition, social

appendix

 C

competence, and self care through the delivery of individualized and comprehensive supports and services.

DEC recognizes that the family is the constant in the life of a child and the purpose of early intervention is to enhance the capacity of the family to facilitate their child's development. Children aged birth to eight spend most of their time with their family or other care givers. Early intervention and early childhood special education services should be designed in response to the concerns and priorities of each family as related to the development of their child, and service delivery should reflect a respect for each family's uniqueness and family system. Service providers should respond to families within the cultural context of both family and community. Similarly, culturally competent community based service systems should be designed to support the participation of children representing the full range of diversity; diversity not only of ethnicity, economics, language, and culture, but of ability as well.

DEC supports the rights of all children, regardless of their diverse abilities, to participate actively in natural environments within their community. A natural environment is one in which a child would spend time if he or she did not have special needs. Family-centered and community based care means that service providers not only provide support for children, but they provide support to families and those in the community as well. Service providers should be able to facilitate parent-to-parent connections and link young children and their families to community-based natural supports such as babysitters, play groups, and libraries. Instead of providing direct supports and services only to young children and their families, service providers should also serve as consultants, coordinators, advocates, facilitators, and team members with community providers.

DEC believes that there is a particular need to develop personnel standards that support the practice of serving all young children in natural and inclusive early childhood settings. While acknowledging that related service personnel, early interventionists, and early childhood special educators will require training within their particular disciplines, we believe that there is a common core of knowledge that all such professionals should possess. In addition, early childhood educators should also possess a core of knowledge about serving children with special needs.

Certification standards should be developed to ensure not only that service providers possess the high degree of specialization that their discipline requires, but also to guarantee that service providers from all disciplines possess the common core of knowledge and skills they need in order to work with young children with special needs in inclusive settings.

DEC is aware of the complex needs of young children with special needs and their families. It is highly unlikely that any individual professional or agency will be able to address all of the needs of children and families. A coordinated and collaborative approach is needed to ensure the availability of comprehensive supports and services by families. The delivery of coordinated supports and services requires a commitment to a common framework of operation guided by a philosophical foundation of collaboration. In many instances, this means the design of new service structures and models of personnel

. . . .

Permission to copy not required—distribution encouraged.

deployment across a variety of disciplines. It also requires that personnel have the requisite knowledge and skills to work with individuals from other professional disciplines and engage in collaborative efforts. Within programs, this means collaborative teamwork skills in assessment and intervention. Across programs, this means collaborative abilities to coordinate and integrate services. DEC believes that policy makers, institutions of higher education, professional organizations and other sources of technical assistance, and local service delivery systems share responsibility for ensuring that services from a variety of disciplines are available and are delivered in a collaborative and integrated manner.

DEC believes that the complex needs of families are best met when every family has access to a service coordinator who becomes a partner with them as they seek appropriate supports and services for themselves and their child. In some cases this coordination role is best met by the family themselves. The coordinator's role is to support families in identifying and obtaining the supports and services (both formal and informal) they want. The service coordinator, to the extent that each family desires, can assist all family members in obtaining the skills needed during the early childhood years and beyond. As with other service providers, there is a need for a sufficient number of skilled service coordinators who are able to deliver culturally competent services. We believe that members of each and all disciplines share with families a responsibility for advocacy on behalf of children with special needs. However, service coordinators have a special responsibility to identify and eliminate gaps in the service system, thus developing a model of service integration for individual families, as well as the service delivery system in general.

DEC believes that great strides continue to be made toward meeting the needs of infants and young children with special needs and their families. While appreciating and honoring the effort resulting in these gains, we also recognize that many children and families remain unserved or under served, and that ensuring that services and supports are of the highest quality remains a challenge. We recognize the responsibility that DEC and its members have in working toward services that are sufficient in both availability and quality to meet the needs of all young children who have disabilities or developmental delays, are at-risk for delay, or are gifted and talented.

Reference

DEC Task Force on Recommended Practices. (1993). *DEC recommended practices: Indicators of quality in programs for infants and young children with special needs and their families.* Reston, VA: Council for Exceptional Children.

THE DIVISION FOR EARLY CHILDHOOD

Division for Early Childhood (DEC) Position on Interventions for Challenging Behavior

ADOPTED: April, 1998

Many young children engage in challenging behavior in the course of early development. The majority of these children respond to developmentally appropriate management techniques.

Every parent, including parents of young children with disabilities, wants his or her child to attend schools, child-care centers, or community-based programs that are nurturing and safe. Many young children engage in challenging behavior at various times during their early development. Typically, this behavior is short-term and decreases with age and use of appropriate guidance strategies. However, for some children these incidences of challenging behavior may become more consistent despite increased adult vigilance and use of appropriate guidance strategies. For these children, the challenging behavior may result in injury to themselves or others, cause damage to the physical environment, interfere with the acquisition of new skills, and/or socially isolate the child (Doss & Reichle, 1991). Additional intervention efforts may by required for these children.

DEC believes strongly that many types of services and intervention strategies are available to address challenging behavior.

Given the developmental nature of most challenging behavior, we believe that there is a vast array of supplemental services that can be added to the home and education environment to increase the likelihood that children will learn appropriate behavior. A variety of intervention strategies can be implemented with either formal or informal support. Services and strategies could include, but are not limited to: (a) designing environments and activities to prevent challenging behavior and to help all children develop appropriate behavior; (b) utilizing effective behavioral interventions that are positive and address both form and function of a young child's challenging behavior; (c) adopting curricular modification and accommodation strategies designed to help young children learn behaviors appropriate to their settings; and (d) providing external consultation and technical assistance or additional staff support. In addition, all professionals who work with children in implementing IEPs or IFSPs must have opportunities to acquire knowledge and skills necessary for effective implementation of prevention and intervention programs.

Permission to copy not required—distribution encouraged.

DEC believes strongly that families play a critical role in designing and carrying out effective interventions for challenging behavior.

Given the family-focused nature of early childhood education, we acknowledge the critical role that families play in addressing challenging behavior. Oftentimes, challenging behavior occurs across places, people, and time, thus families are critical members of the intervention team. A coordinated effort between family members and professionals is needed to ensure that interventions are effective and efficient and address both child and family needs and strengths. All decisions regarding the identification of a challenging behavior, possible interventions, placement, and ongoing evaluation must be made in accordance with the family through the IEP, IFSP, or other team decision-making processes.

Reference

Doss, L.S. & Reichle, J. (1991). Replacing excess behavior with an initial communicative repertoire. In J. Reichle, J. York, & J. Sigafoos (Eds.), *Implementing augmentative and alternative communication: Strategies for learners with severe disabilities*. Baltimore: Paul H. Brooks.

Permission to copy not required—distribution encouraged.

THE DIVISION FOR EARLY CHILDHOOD

Division for Early Childhood (DEC) Concept Paper on the Identification of and Intervention With Challenging Behavior

ADOPTED by DEC Executive Board: October 4, 1999

ENDORSED: National Association for the Education of Young Children, November 1999
Association for Childhood Education International, November 1999

Many young children engage in challenging behavior in the course of early development. The majority of these children respond to developmentally appropriate management techniques.

Many young children, including children with disabilities, engage in behavior that is labeled by adults as "challenging." Sometimes, this behavior is short-term and decreases with age and use of appropriate guidance strategies. Additionally, what is "challenging" to one person may not be to another. It is critical for professionals to be aware of and sensitive to how families, cultural groups, and communities define appropriate and inappropriate behavior in young children. Different communities have varying expectations for child behavior. Professionals must respect family, cultural, and community expectations in identifying problems and designing interventions. However, sometimes families or professionals may have inappropriate expectations for young children's behavior. It is important to understand what behaviors are typically associated with particular age groups. For instance, adults need to understand that young children engage in behaviors that older children do not, such as throwing toys or sitting for only short periods of time. With guidance and instruction most children will learn appropriate alternative behavior. Adults must also explore their own beliefs and emotions about certain behaviors (e.g., cursing or hurting others) in order to respond objectively to children. In summary, care must be taken to consider cultural and community beliefs, developmentally appropriate expectations, and one's own beliefs about behavior in the identification of children's behavior as "challenging."

Regrettably, some children's challenging behaviors are not effectively addressed by adult vigilance and use of appropriate guidance strategies. For these children, the challenging behavior may result in injury to themselves or others, cause damage to the physical environment, interfere with the acquisition of new skills, and/or socially isolate the child (Doss & Reichle, 1989; Kaiser & Rasminsky, 1999). It is clear that challenging behaviors such as these seldom resolve themselves without systematic intervention (Kazdin, 1987; Olweus, 1979; Wahler & Dumas, 1986). Relatedly, there is growing evidence that many young children who engage in chronic, highly challenging behaviors proceed through a

appendix
C

predictable course of ever-escalating challenging behaviors (Patterson & Bank, 1989; Reid, 1993). What intervention efforts are available for a child who engages in serious challenging behavior?

DEC believes strongly that many types of services and intervention strategies are available to address challenging behavior.

Children may well engage in challenging behavior that quite often can be eliminated by a change in adult behavior. It is possible that the child is reacting to adult behaviors such as lack of attention or unrealistic expectations. By changing adult behavior, we may *prevent* a child's need to engage in challenging behavior. Prevention is the best form of intervention (Poulsen, 1993; Zirpoli & Melloy, 1993). It is time and cost-efficient, and appears to be a major avenue by which to eliminate, not merely reduce, the incidence of challenging behaviors (Strain, Steele, Ellis, & Timm, 1982). Prevention means that the important adults in the child's life have to look at their own behavior in the classroom, home, or community setting that might be maintaining the child's challenging behaviors (McEvoy, Fox, & Rosenberg, 1991; Strain & Hemmeter, 1997). For example, are toddlers expected to sit through a 30-minute circle time? Is a child getting a cookie when he or she screams? Effective prevention strategies that have been applied to the challenging behaviors of young children have included systematic efforts to teach parents to use child behavior management skills (Timm, 1993) and efforts to teach alternative, appropriate behaviors that are coordinated between programs *and* home (Walker, Stiller, & Golly, 1998).

Given the nature of most challenging behavior, we believe that there is a vast array of supplemental services that can be added to the home and early education environment to increase the likelihood that children will learn appropriate behavior. A variety of intervention strategies can be implemented with either formal or informal support. Services and strategies could include, but are not limited to: (a) designing environments and activities to prevent challenging behavior and to help all children develop appropriate behavior; (b) utilizing effective behavioral interventions that are positive and that address both the form and function of a young child's challenging behavior; (c) adopting curricular modification and accommodation strategies designed to help young children learn behaviors appropriate to their settings; and (d) providing external consultation and technical assistance or additional staff support (e.g. with appropriately trained early childhood special educators). In addition, all professionals who work with children in implementing Individualized Education Programs (IEPs) or Individualized Family Service Plans (IFSPs) must have opportunities to acquire knowledge and skills necessary for effective implementation of prevention and intervention programs.

Family members and professionals should work together to identify the challenging behavior, assess it in the settings where it occurs, and design interventions that are realistic to implement and empirically sound. There are literally dozens of empirically validated interventions designed to decrease the challenging behaviors of young children. Effective interventions include the following features:

appendix
C

Comprehensive—It is seldom the case that one intervention strategy will be sufficiently powerful to yield a satisfactory change in challenging behaviors. Therefore, *a comprehensive approach* is highly recommended. For example, a preschool teacher may find that a comprehensive intervention package comprised of the following strategies for teaching children to share will yield far more favorable outcomes than any one strategy used in isolation: a) adaptations to activities—a part of opening circle and storytime is devoted to teaching sharing skills; b) rehearsal of class rules—sharing is added to class rules and children are reminded of all rules prior to each class transition; c) role-playing alternative behaviors— from a prevention perspective, all children are given opportunities to practice sharing and other class rules at the end of opening circle and at the beginning of storytime and from an intervention perspective, squabbles over toys and materials are responded to by having the parties practice appropriate sharing; d) arranging for peer models/reinforcing desirable behaviors—many times throughout the day, all children could be found following all class rules, including sharing. When sharing is observed, the teacher communicates in a very positive and public fashion about who is sharing and how they are sharing.

Individualized—Like all other areas of intervention programming, *individualization* is key to success with challenging behaviors. While there is great appeal to the simple formula approach to challenging behaviors (e.g., if Sally does this behavior, you do this), it is a formula doomed to failure. There is overwhelming evidence that children do the same challenging behaviors (e.g., screaming) for fundamentally different reasons *and* that they may also engage in completely different challenging behaviors (e.g., running away, hitting peers) for the same reason (Carr & Durand, 1985). Therefore, it is imperative to know, at the individual child and specific behavior level, the probable motivations or functions for the challenging acts. For example, a child may scream and cry because she wants more attention, or because she does not want to do something asked of her. The "form" of the behavior is crying. But there are two possible "functions" described above (attention and escape) that would require different interventions. When choosing an intervention it is critical to assess both what (form) the behavior is and why (function) the child is exhibiting the behavior [see O'Neill, Horner, Albin, Storey, & Sprague (1990) for in-depth descriptions of methods used to identify the specific communicative intent or function of challenging behaviors]. Once this assessment process is complete, an individualized set of strategies can be developed and implemented.

Positive Programming—Because many challenging behaviors elicit such strong emotional responses and at times poor behavior choices by caregivers and teachers, it is essential to focus on the *positive* aspects of programming (Neilsen, Olive, Donovan, & McEvoy, 1998). Positive programming refers to: (a) teaching appropriate social skills (e.g., entering play groups), (b) teaching children to self-evaluate and self-monitor their behavior (e.g., am I saying nice things?), and (c) teaching specific communicative *alternatives* to challenging behaviors (teaching a child who tantrums at clean up time to sign or say "more"). This positive, teaching focus also reflects the now accepted and empirically-validated notion that many challenging behaviors stem directly from lack of skill in the social and communicative domains.

Multi-Disciplinary—It is also the case that the challenging behaviors of some children clearly demand the input and expertise of *multiple disciplines*. Early childhood special educators, early childhood educators, and psychologists are typical members of a team. Pediatricians, neurologists, and child psychiatrists, for example, can also play useful roles in those complex instances in which the child's challenging behaviors have a known or suspected neurobiological basis (Hirshberg, 1997/1998). The speech therapist is an essential member of the intervention team when the behavior may be a result of frustration with speech/language difficulties. The role of a team approach is crucial. Just as it is unlikely that a singular educational intervention will be sufficient to manage serious challenging behaviors, it is also unlikely that a biomedical or pharmacological or some other intervention alone will be sufficient.

Data-Based—A reliable, viable, and useful system of *data collection* is essential to the success of any intervention plan (Kaiser & Rasminsky, 1999). Data collection can serve many purposes specifically related to challenging behavior. As we indicated above, challenging behaviors often elicit strong, emotional responses from the adults in a child's life. These responses make it difficult for us to be objective about the severity or frequency of a challenging behavior and also can prevent us from recognizing a child's progress related to the challenging behavior. For example, a teacher or parent may be struggling to reduce the spitting behavior of a young boy. The child spits when apparently happy, upset, or angry, or when hugged or when scolded. When the behavioral consultant asks how often the child spits, the answer is "all the time." In fact, the child is observed to spit 70 to 100 times per day, or put differently, he spits for less than 2 minutes in the four-hour data collection period. To adults this level of spitting indeed feels like "all the time." However, the data collection details the actual frequency as well as other important facts. Data collection can assist us in identifying the frequency of the challenging behavior, contextual variables that may be supporting the child's challenging behavior, and changes that may be needed in the environment to reduce the occurrences of the challenging behavior. In addition, data collection can be used to determine the extent to which an intervention or change in the environment is having a positive effect on the child's behavior. Finally, a data collection system, if designed correctly, increases the likelihood that the adults across the child's environments are addressing the challenging behavior in a consistent way.

DEC believes strongly that families play a critical role in designing and carrying out effective interventions for challenging behavior.

Given the family-focused nature of early childhood education, we acknowledge the central role that families play in addressing challenging behavior. Oftentimes, challenging behavior occurs across places, people, and time; thus families are critical members of the intervention team. A coordinated effort between family members and professionals is needed to assure that interventions are effective and efficient and address both child and family needs and strengths. All decisions regarding the identification of a challenging

appendix

C

behavior, possible interventions, placement, and ongoing evaluation must be made in accordance with the family through the IEP, IFSP, or other team decision-making processes.

Often, families are *blamed* for a child's problem behavior. In an extensive review of the literature concerning families of preschool children with conduct problems, Webster-Stratton (1997) confirmed that certain parental/family factors including depression, substance abuse, aggression, antisocial behavior, intense marital conflict, insularity, and ineffective parenting skills appear related to the presence of behavior problems for some children. However, a growing body of evidence was cited in which other factors such as child physiological/neurological/neuropsychological attributes, communication competence, child social problem-solving skill deficiencies, family poverty, and school setting characteristics also appear directly related to the presence or absence of challenging behavior in children. The most promising emerging perspective within this literature emphasizes the complex interplay among risk factors leading to the formation and perpetuation of problem behaviors.

While the family may or may not have contributed directly to the creation of the challenging behavior, family members are almost always *significantly affected* by the behavior. Webster-Stratton (1990) found that families of children with serious behavioral problems reported the presence of major stressors in their lives two to four times more frequently than did families with typically developing children. Family members are likely to receive unsolicited advice with every tantrum, outburst, and misbehavior. Activities that other families seem to enjoy as a matter of course are unattainable or are in constant jeopardy. Isolation becomes a fact of life.

As described earlier, families of children with challenging behavior require access to a *range* of intervention services that are *coordinated* to meet their specific needs. Nicholas Hobbs (1982) observed that "The way one defines a problem will determine in substantial measure the strategies that can be used to solve it" (p. 182). Obviously, if a preponderance of researchers, policy-makers, and practitioners are convinced that families deserve blame for the existence of most challenging behavior, then available services will be structured accordingly. But even if the question of blame is eliminated, there is reason to be concerned that other differences in professional beliefs regarding challenging behavior can create comparable difficulties for families. Advocates of psychopharmacological versus behavioral interventions, homeopathic versus traditional medical treatments, family-centered versus child-centered approaches, or center-based versus home-based service delivery systems collectively produce a bewildering array of disjointed information and difficult choices. Many families of children with challenging behavior have astounding stories to tell regarding their journeys through this landscape of conflicting diagnoses, bickering professionals, and expensive mistakes. There are some children whose problematic behavior is controlled most immediately by physiological factors. There are some individuals who might benefit from appropriate psychopharmacological treatment in order to respond to complementary environmental, curricular, or behavioral interventions. Therefore, as noted earlier, professionals must be aware of the various disciplines and services that might serve as appropriate resources to the family (Reichle et al., 1996). All professionals have a fundamental obligation to provide accurate information and support to families as multiple approaches and options are considered.

Finally, families need *partners*. Dunst, Trivette, and Deal (1988) proposed that within the working relationship involving families and early intervention professionals "It is not simply a matter of whether family needs are met, but rather the manner in which needs are met that is likely to be both enabling and empowering" (p. 4). Parents of children with challenging behavior are often frustrated with the child, other family members, and themselves. The understanding and support of professionals can have a profound and positive impact. They need effective tools to use, appropriate resources for support, and reassurance that they and their child are accepted.

Professionals and families must carefully evaluate a child's behavior. The focus must be on promoting positive behavior and preventing challenging behaviors. In the appropriate identification of challenging behaviors, consideration must be taken of cultural and community beliefs, developmentally appropriate expectations, and an examination of one's own belief about behavior. When intervention is needed, such interventions must be developmentally, individually, and culturally appropriate. They should be comprehensive, individualized, positive, and multi-disciplinary and should consider families as integral to all decisions related to the planning and implementation of the strategies and services.

This concept paper is the result of a work group of DEC members: Linda Brault, Judy Carta, Mary Louise Hemmeter, Mary McEvoy, Shelley Neilsen, Beth Rous, Barbara Smith, Phil Strain, and Matt Timm.

References

Carr, E.G., & Durand, V.M. (1985). Reducing problem behaviors through functional communication training. *Journal of Applied Behavior Analysis, 18*, 111-126.

Doss, L.S., & Reichle, J. (1989). Establishing communicative alternatives to the emissions of socially motivated excess behavior: A review. *Journal of the Association for Persons with Severe Handicaps, 14*, 101-112.

Dunst, C., Trivette, C., & Deal, A. (1988). *Enabling and empowering parents.* Cambridge, MA: Brookline.

Hirshberg, L.M. (1997/1998). Infant mental health consultation to early intervention programs. *Zero to Three, 18*(3) 19-23.

Hobbs, N. (1982). *The troubled and troubling child.* San Francisco: Jossey-Bass.

Kazdin, A. (1987). *Conduct disorders in childhood.* Newbury Park, CA: Sage.

Kaiser, B., & Rasminsky, J.S. (1999). *Meeting the challenge: Effective strategies for challenging behaviors in early childhood environments.* Washington, DC: NAEYC.

McEvoy, M.A., Fox, J.J., & Rosenberg, M.S. (1991). Organizing preschool environments: Effects on the behavior of preschool children with handicaps. *Education and Treatment of Children, 14*, 18-28.

Neilsen, S., Olive, M., Donovan, A., & McEvoy, M. (1998). Challenging behavior in your classroom? Don't react, teach instead! *Young Exceptional Children, 2*(1), 2-10.

Olweus, D. (1979). Stability of aggressive reaction patterns in males: A review. *Psychological Bulletin, 86*, 852-875.

appendix
C

O'Neill, R.E., Horner, R.H., Albin, R.W., Storey, K., & Sprague, J.R. (1990). *Functional analysis: A practical assessment guide.* Pacific Grove, CA: Brooks/Cole.

Patterson, G.R., & Bank, L. (1989). Some amplifying mechanisms for pathological processes in families. In M.R. Gunnar & E. Thelen (Eds.), *Systems and development: The Minnesota symposia on child psychology* (Vol. 22, pp. 167- 209). Hillsdale, NJ: Erlbaum.

Poulsen, M.K. (1993). Strategies for building resilience in infants and young children at risk. *Infants and Young Children, 6*(2) 29-40.

Reichle, J., McEvoy, M., Davis, C., Feeley, K., Johnston, S., & Wolff, K. (1996). Coordinating preservice and inservice training of early interventionists to serve preschoolers who engage in challenging behavior. In R. Koegel, L. Koegel, & G. Dunlap. (Eds), *Positive behavioral support* (pp. 227-264). Baltimore, MD: Paul H. Brooks.

Reid, J. (1993). Prevention of conduct disorder before and after school entry: Relating interventions to developmental findings. *Development and Psychopathology, 5,* 243-262.

Strain, P.S., & Hemmeter, M.L. (1997). Keys to being successful when confronted with challenging behaviors. *Young Exceptional Children, 1*(1), 2-9.

Strain, P.S., Steele, P., Ellis, T., & Timm, M.A. (1982). Long-term effects of oppositional child treatment with mothers as therapists and therapist trainers. *Journal of Applied Behavior Analysis, 15,* 163-169.

Timm, M.A. (1993). The Regional Intervention Program. *Behavioral Disorders, 19,* 34- 43.

Wahler, R., & Dumas, J.E. (1986). "A chip off the old block:" Some interpersonal characteristics of coercive children across generations. In P. Strain, M. Guralnick, & H.M. Walker (Eds.), *Children's social behavior: Development, assessment and modification* (pp. 49-91). Orlando, FL: Academic Press.

Walker, H.M., Stiller, B., & Golly, A. (1998). First steps to success. *Young Exceptional Children, 1,* 2-7.

Webster-Stratton, C. (1990). Stress: A potential disruptor of parent perceptions and family interactions. *Journal of Clinical Child Psychology, 19,* 302-312.

Webster-Stratton, C. (1997). Early intervention for families of preschool children with conduct problems. In M. Guralnick (Ed.), *The effectiveness of early interventions* (pp. 429-453). Baltimore, MD: Paul H. Brookes.

Zirpoli, T.J., & Melloy, K.J. (1993). *Behavior management: Applications for teachers and parents.* New York: Merrill.

appendix
C

THE DIVISION FOR EARLY CHILDHOOD

Code of Ethics

The Division for Early Childhood
of the Council for Exceptional Children

Adopted: September, 1996
Revised: April, 1999

As members of the Division for Early Childhood (DEC) of the Council for Exceptional Children (CEC), we recognize that in our professional conduct we are faced with choices that call on us to determine right from wrong. Other choices, however, are not nearly as clear, forcing us to choose between competing priorities and to acknowledge the moral ambiguity of life. The following code of ethics is based on the Division's recognition of the critical role of conscience not merely in preventing wrong, but in choosing among courses of action in order to act in the best interests of young children with special needs and their families and to support our professional colleagues.

As members of DEC, we acknowledge our responsibility to abide by high standards of performance and ethical conduct and we commit to:

1. Demonstrate the highest standards of personal integrity, truthfulness, and honesty in all our professional activities in order to inspire the confidence and trust of the public and those with whom we work;

2. Demonstrate our respect and concern for children and families, colleagues, and others with whom we work, honoring their beliefs, values, customs, and culture;

3. Demonstrate our respect for families in their task of nurturing their children, and support them in achieving the outcomes they desire for themselves and their children;

4. Demonstrate, in our behavior and language, that we respect and appreciate the unique value and human potential of each child;

5. Strive for personal professional excellence, seeking new information, using new information and ideas, and responding openly to the suggestions of others;

6. Encourage the professional development of our colleagues and those seeking to enter fields related to early childhood special education, early intervention, and personnel preparation, offering guidance, assistance, support, and mentorship to others without the burden of professional competition;

7. Ensure that programs and services we provide are based on law as well as a current knowledge of and recommended practice in early childhood special education, early intervention, and personnel preparation;

appendix

C

8. Serve as an advocate for children with special needs and their families and for the professionals who serve them in our communities, working with those who make the policy and programmatic decisions that enhance or depreciate the quality of their lives;

9. Oppose any discrimination because of race, color, religion, sex, sexual orientation, national origin, political affiliation, disability, age, or marital status in all aspects of personnel action and service delivery;

10. Protect the privacy and confidentiality of information regarding children and families, colleagues, and students; and

11. Reflect our commitment to the Division for Early Childhood and to its adopted policies and positions.

The Division for Early Childhood acknowledges with appreciation the National Association for the Education of Young Children, the American Society for Public Administration, and the Council for Exceptional Children, whose codes of conduct were helpful as we developed our own.

Appendix D

Glossary

. . . .

Assistive technology. Any item, piece of equipment, or product, whether acquired commercially, off the shelf, modified, or customized, that is used to increase, maintain, or improve the functional capabilities of individuals with disabilities. Also includes instructional technology.

Caregivers. The people who spend significant amounts of time with the child, such as parents, child care providers, and teachers.

Collaboration. Working with others to accomplish shared, identified goals and cooperating willingly.

Culture. Broadly defined to include beliefs, values, and traditions associated with race, ethnicity, language, and social and economic circumstances.

Curriculum-based assessment. A measure in which an individual child's performance is compared with a sequence of curricular objectives.

Disability and/or developmental delay. Terms have different definitions under different state and federal policies; for purposes of this book, disability and developmental delay mean the conditions used to determine eligibility under IDEA:

- Part C of IDEA: Infants and toddlers with disabilities means children from birth through age 2 who need early intervention services because they (1) are experiencing developmental delay, as measured by appropriate diagnostic instruments and procedures, in one or more of the following areas: cognitive development, physical development including vision and hearing, communication development, social or emotional development, adaptive development; or (2) have a diagnosed physical or mental condition that has a high probability of resulting in developmental delay (examples of these conditions include chromosomal abnormalities; genetic or congenital disorders; severe sensory impairments, including hearing and vision; inborn errors of metabolism; disorders reflecting disturbance of the development of the nervous system; congenital infections; disorders secondary to exposure to toxic substances including fetal alcohol syndrome; and severe attachment disorders). The term may also include, at a State's discretion, children from birth through age 2 who are at risk of having substantial developmental delays if early intervention services are not provided. States may include well-known biological and environmental factors that can be identified and that place infants and toddlers "at risk" for developmental delay. Commonly cited risk factors include low birth weight, respiratory distress as a newborn, lack of oxygen, brain hemorrhage, infection, nutritional deprivation, and a history of abuse or neglect.

● **Part B of IDEA:** The term child with a disability means a child aged 3-21 appropriately evaluated as having mental retardation, a hearing impairment including deafness, a speech or language impairment, a visual impairment including blindness, serious emotional disturbance, an orthopedic impairment, autism, traumatic brain injury, another health impairment, a specific learning disability, deaf-blindness, or multiple disabilities and who, by reason thereof, needs special education and related services.

The term child with a disability for children aged 3–9 may, at the discretion of the State and local school district, include a child (1) who is experiencing developmental delays, as defined by the State and as measured by appropriate diagnostic instruments and procedures, in one or more of the following areas: physical development, cognitive development, communication development, social or emotional development, or adaptive development; and (2) who, by reason thereof, needs special education and related services.

Distance education. Refers to a system in which educator and learner are separated by physical distance; the concept is that distance education systems may bring together, in virtual space, learners, educators, and curriculum materials that are distributed throughout a wide arena.

Early Intervention (EI). Refers to services and supports for children under the age of 3 years.

Early Childhood Special Education (ECSE). Refers to services and supports for children ages 3–5 years.

Engagement. The child's interacting with the environment in a developmentally and contextually appropriate manner.

Family. Two or more individuals, one of whom is an adult and the other a child, who are bound to each other through birth, adoption, or guardianship. Every family is different, and families define themselves differently.

Family centered. Approach to EI/ECSE that recognizes the family as the constant in the child's life, respects the family's central role in the development of the child, and respects the family's role in decision making.

FAPE. Free Appropriate Public Education under IDEA.

High technology. Usually refers to complex electrical and electronic devices, such as computers, voice synthesizers, Braille readers, augmentative communication systems, and environmental control units.

IEP. Individualized Education Program—a written plan for services for children ages 3–21 with disabilities under IDEA. If allowed under state and local policy, children 3–5 may have an IFSP instead of an IEP with informed parental consent.

IFSP. Individualized Family Services Plan—a written plan for services for birth through 2-year olds with disabilities under IDEA. If allowed under state and local policy, children 3–5 may have an IFSP instead of an IEP with informed parental consent.

Interagency. Between agencies; usually refers to agencies that provide services and supports to children and families.

Inservice. The process of providing ongoing professional development for professionals and paraprofessionals, with the outcome being enhanced professional practice.

Least restrictive environment. According to IDEA: To the maximum extent appropriate, children with disabilities, including children in public or private institutions or other care facilities, are educated with children who are nondisabled. Further, special classes, separate schooling, or other removal of children with disabilities from the regular educational environment occurs only if the nature or severity of the disability is such that education in regular classes with the use of supplementary aids and services cannot be achieved satisfactorily.

Low technology. Refers to more simple (than high technology) devices; supports; systems; and adaptations such as custom-designed hand tools, positioning devices, and other simple, inexpensive, easy-to-use devices.

Natural environments. A setting in which the child would spend time had he or she not had a disability.

Norm-referenced assessment. A measure in which an individual child's performance is compared with that of a normative group, usually of others of the same age.

Normalized intervention strategies. Educational/developmental methods that are similar to those provided to typically developing children.

Paraeducator. A trained person who assists a certified educator as an aide.

Paraprofessional. A trained person who assists a certified or licensed professional as an aide (includes paraeducators).

appendix **D**

Preservice. Refers to postsecondary programs at the 2-year, 4-year, or graduate level that lead to entry-level preparation in the field of study and result in a degree and/or licensure in that field.

Services coordination. Activities carried out to assist and enable a child and family to receive the rights, procedural safeguards, and services that are authorized to be provided.

Service coordinator. An individual who acts as the coordinator of a child's and family's services and works in partnership with the family.

Social relationships. The product of long-term reciprocal interactions between children.

Stakeholders. Individuals who have a stake or interest in services.

Supplementary aids and services. According to IDEA: Supplementary aids and services means aids, services, and other supports that are provided in regular education classes or other education-related settings to the child or on behalf of the child to enable children with disabilities to be educated with nondisabled children to the maximum extent appropriate in accordance with the LRE requirements.

Zero reject. All eligible children receive a free and appropriate public education (FAPE) under IDEA.

DEC Recommended Practices Program Assessment
Improving Practices for Young Children with Special Needs and Their Families

On the heels of *DEC Recommended Practices in Early Intervention/Early Childhood Special Education*, comes this important next step. The *Program Assessment* will provide you with a reliable method of evaluating, and ultimately, improving, your current program for young children with special needs.

Through this process, you will:

- Understand your program's strengths, uncover its flaws, and know when to make changes in administrative policies and direct services
- Be able to identify professional development priorities
- Have the tools to measure the impact of training, technical assistance, and other program improvement strategies
- The Program Assessment includes a rating scale, summary form, an action planning form, and a progress form. Examples and case studies are used to clarify specific practices and their implementation.

Expected publication: December 2001
Call Sopris West at (800) 547-6747 for ordering information

To order more copies of *DEC Recommended Practices in Early Intervention/Early Childhood Special Education*, contact:

yOung Exceptional children

Monograph Series

Monograph No. 1: Practical Ideas for Addressing Challenging Behaviors

These articles, gathered from *Young Exceptional Children*, offer proven interventions with challenging behaviors that can be used in early childhood programs and at home. Articles cover such topics as identification, prevention, environmental modifications, instruction of appropriate alternative behaviors, and more. You'll gain positive practices for helping children: stay on task, transition to the next activity, learn positive social interactions, gain attending skills, and communicate wants and needs appropriately.

Research-based strategies, written in accessible language, are accompanied by examples of how strategies can be implemented in real-life situations in early childhood programs and at home.

Monograph No. 2: Natural Environments and Inclusion

With IDEA '97 prompting inclusive settings for children with disabilities, it is important to consider the natural settings in which these children are being taught and cared for—child-care centers and preschools in particular.

The articles in *Natural Environments and Inclusion* focus on important issues, suggesting ways to help children and their families successfully participate in natural settings. You'll find strategies to help you effectively implement the itinerant teaching model used with preschool children, as well as answers to a variety of questions providers and families ask regarding changes in early intervention. You'll learn why planning is so important and how to support preschoolers as they participate in a wide variety of activities and settings within an inclusive classroom.

Monograph No. 3: Teaching Strategies

The focus of this latest issue will be on effective and doable teaching strategies that teachers can use in their early childhood classrooms or centers. Articles will highlight teaching practices for a variety of curriculum content. (Expected publication December 2001)

Four Easy Ways to Order

Fax Toll Free
(888) 819-7767

Phone Toll Free
(800) 547-6747

Mail to
Sopris West
4093 Specialty Place
Longmont, CO 80504

Internet
www.sopriswest.com

SOPRIS WEST

Prod. Code	Product Title	Qty.	Unit Price	Total Price
G143MONO1	YEC Monograph No. 1: *Practical Ideas for Addressing Challenging Behaviors*	_____	$ 12.00	_____
G143MONO2	YEC Monograph No. 2: *Natural Environments and Inclusion*	_____	$ 12.00	_____
G143MONO3	YEC Monograph No. 3: *Teaching Strategies*	_____	$ 12.00	_____

Subtotal _____

Shipping & Handling (add 10%) _____

CO residents please add 3% sales tax. _____

TOTAL _____

Name _____

Job Title _____

Grades I Work With _____

School/Institution _____

District _____

Street _____

City/State/Zip _____

Phone_____

Fax _____

Email _____

This address is: ❑ School/Institution ❑ Home
May we email you about related resources? ❑ Yes ❑ No

Method of Payment

❑ Check (made out to Sopris West)

❑ PO (must be signed and faxed or mailed with order)

❑ MC   ❑ Visa

Card Number:
_____

Expiration Date_____

Print Name of Cardholder:
_____

Cardholder Signature:
_____